Number at Key Stage 2

core materials for teaching and assessing number and algebra

Mike Askew, Rob Briscoe,
Sheila Ebbutt, Lynda Maple
and Fran Mosley

Copyright © BEAM 1996
Cover illustration © Beverly Levy, 12 Shipton Street, London E2 7RU
Photographs on page iii and opposite pages 15, 29, 43, 99, 113, 127 © Sally and
Richard Greenhill, 357A Liverpool Road, London N1 1NL; photographs opposite
pages 57, 71 by Elizabeth Wright for Orangebox; other photographs by Len Cross

ISBN 1 874099 31 6
Designed and typeset by Bookcraft, 9 Lower Street, Stroud GL5 2HT
Printed by Five Castles Press, Duke Street, Ipswich, IP3 0AG

Tower Hamlets

KING'S
College
LONDON
Founded 1829

ISLINGTON COUNCIL

Contents

INTRODUCTION

The need for this book

This book offers a set of core activities around which to base your scheme of work for number. We have not intended to provide an entire number curriculum at key stage 2 — you will need to supplement our suggestions with your own favourites, practice material, pages from published material, and so on. But we have tried to offer one set of activities for each important strand of number at this level.

This book grew out of the work done by a group of teachers who were attending a course at King's College, London on developing a scheme of work for number. The teachers who produced the original scheme had something that they could use in school. But when this scheme was trialled with other teachers it became apparent that they found it difficult to implement — they had not been through the process of developing the scheme for themselves and so did not 'own' it in any way. A further period of trialling, reshaping and rewriting was necessary.

Thinking about what had happened, it occurred to us that all over the country teachers with responsibility for mathematics were working on schemes of work for their schools. While it is important that teachers and schools are active in developing a scheme they feel comfortable with, it also seems unnecessary for everyone to have to keep reinventing the wheel. Hence this publication, which provides core activities, tried and tested and rewritten as needed, for schools to use as a basis around which to build a scheme they can truly own.

The contents of the book

'Pupils should be given opportunities to: develop flexible and effective methods of computation and recording; use calculators computers and a range of resources.'
Programme of Study for Number at Key Stage 2

The book contains ten sections, broadly corresponding to the programmes of study for number at key stage 2. It is important that children work in a variety of ways, using a variety of tools, and for this reason each section, except for Applying Operations, contains activities using the same six tools: mental methods; number lines, cards and grids; calculators; computers; objects such as base ten blocks or counters; pencil and paper. So, for instance, in the section on Decimals there are six activities which use the range of tools described above. This means that in planning a teaching session you have a choice of activities and can choose which tool you prefer to use at that moment — linking cubes because they are familiar, calculators because they aren't familiar, number lines because you want to introduce children to number lines and this is a good way to do it . . .

Another important feature of these activities is that they are designed to be adapted for children working at different levels of attainment. Nearly all the activities can be used with children who are working within level 2 right through to those working within level 5. The grid at the beginning of each section shows the names of the six activities in that section and indicates what attainment levels they are suitable for.

The six tools

There is no one best way of teaching mathematics. Children respond differently to experiences, and what works for one may not work for another. In order to help children become confident in number they need a broad and balanced curriculum within mathematics itself. They need access to mathematical ideas through a variety of experiences without any particular way of working being dominant. To help achieve this breadth and balance we suggest that children are offered six sorts of experience to embody mathematics.

● *Mental mathematics*

Learning mathematics is ultimately a mental activity. No amount of practical work will help children learn unless they abstract the mental mathematics from the experience. This process of abstraction is helped if, from an early age, children are expected to reflect on how they worked something out, to picture things in their heads and to manipulate mental objects. Children can be very inventive with mental calculations, using methods they have never been taught, and making connections they have never made before. Mental mathematics encourages children to use numbers flexibly, and to see patterns and relationships. In order to know how children think about numbers, it is important to discuss, share and compare methods, and to expect children to be explicit about their mental images.

Part of an investigation arising
from work on the activity
Connections (*see page 34*)

● *Lines, cards and grids*

Becoming confident with number involves having a sense of the magnitude of numbers, and having a repertoire of symbolic images to draw upon. Number grids of various types (hundred squares, multiplication and addition squares and so on), number lines, and number cards provide rich sources of activity and also offer children a range of mental images that can support the development of mental strategies. Number lines in particular provide a valuable image of numbers which many adults draw on in everyday mental calculation and estimation.

● *Calculators*

There is now a body of research evidence demonstrating that structured use of calculators helps children's understanding of numbers. Free access to calculators at all stages of schooling can actually lead to improved attainment within the framework of well-planned mathematics teaching. The calculator activities in this book challenge children, encouraging them to predict 'what will happen next' and asking them to work out how the calculator is operating on numbers.

$$\frac{1}{2} \times 1000 = 500$$

$$\frac{1}{2} \times 500 = 250$$

$$1 - \frac{1}{2} - \frac{1}{4} = \frac{1}{4}$$

$$\frac{1}{2} \times 1 \times \frac{1}{2} = \frac{1}{4}$$

$$\frac{1}{2} \times \frac{1}{4} = 1/8$$

On the calculator we did 1/2 × 1/4 which gave us 1/8 and that's a half of a quarter. To find a quarter of a half we did ¼ × ½ which gave us 1/8. So 4/8 makes 1 half. Then we did ¼ × ¼ to find out how much a quarter is, we got 1/16.

$$\frac{1}{4} \times \frac{1}{2} = \frac{1}{8}$$

$$\frac{1}{3} \times \frac{1}{2} = \frac{1}{6}$$

Introduction

• Computers

Working with computers can provide children with valuable learning opportunities that they might not otherwise have. The computer often provides feedback on what the child has done which is impartial and non-judgemental. It does not have the expectations about some children succeeding and others failing which can colour human responses.

The speed of the computer enables children to produce many examples when exploring mathematical problems. This supports them in their observation of patterns and their making of hypotheses and generalisations.

When working with tables and graphs, the computer does the number-crunching, allowing children to focus on mathematical connections.

Children have to be accurate, and to express themselves clearly, when communicating with the computer — whether they are pressing one key or entering a whole set of instructions. The computer cannot interpret and guess at the meaning of unclear instructions in the way that a human can.

• Objects

It is very important that children continue to do some work with practical materials throughout their primary school career, in order to build sound mental models of mathematical relationships. Each section in the book contains one activity using readily available objects. Sometimes these are 'structured' materials — commercially produced material that embodies a particular mathematical idea. Sometimes they are objects that are simply fun to work with and to count — bottle tops, conkers, cubes or beans.

● Pencil and paper

The great advantage of pencil and paper is that they extend our 'mental screens'. Holding several ideas in the head at once is difficult; pencil and paper help children hold onto ideas by recording them, before going on to play with, sort or manipulate them. Paper and pencil methods are not appropriate as ends in themselves, but are useful as means to an end.

Writing a sequence of numbers on a blank number line is a useful assessment activity.

The importance of discussion

Learning mathematics is essentially a social process and comes about through the sharing of ideas. Discussion is therefore central to all the activities in this book: discussion between you and the children, and discussion between the children themselves. In order to make sure that your time spent with children is used fairly you could hold dicussion sessions with the whole class or else split them into groups and timetable yourself to be with each group in turn.

Talking is also a way of lessening the demands on your time. For instance, you can:

- talk through activities with the whole class — children who are not going to do an activity immediately will need less instruction when their turn does come
- get children who have already done an activity to explain it to others
- use reporting-back sessions at the end of lessons to set up further work

Teaching and assessing

While children are involved in learning from the activities in this book you can also assess their levels of attainment. Each activity has a section of questions under the heading 'Can the children . . .'. These questions are graded into four levels, level 2, level 3, level 4 and level 5, and can be used to help you judge what a child can and cannot do, and what they do or do not understand. When planning how to use an activity with children — whether a group

Work on one of the follow-ups to Shade It *(see page 40)*

Lola + Eleanor

$$① \quad 1 = \tfrac{1}{8} + \tfrac{1}{8} + \tfrac{1}{8} + \tfrac{1}{8} + \tfrac{1}{8} + \tfrac{1}{8} + \tfrac{1}{4} = 1$$

$$② \quad \tfrac{1}{2} + \tfrac{1}{2} = 1$$

$$③ \quad \tfrac{1}{8} + \tfrac{1}{8} + \tfrac{1}{8} + \tfrac{1}{8} + \tfrac{1}{4} + \tfrac{1}{4} = 1$$

$$④ \quad \tfrac{1}{4} + \tfrac{1}{4} + \tfrac{1}{4} + \tfrac{1}{4} = 1$$

$$⑤ \quad \tfrac{1}{8} + \tfrac{1}{8} + \tfrac{1}{8} + \tfrac{1}{8} + \tfrac{1}{8} = 1$$

$$⑥ \quad \tfrac{1}{8} + \tfrac{1}{8} + \tfrac{1}{8} + \tfrac{1}{8} + \tfrac{1}{8} + \tfrac{1}{8} + \tfrac{1}{8} + \tfrac{1}{8} = 1$$

$$\tfrac{1}{4} + \tfrac{1}{4}$$

or the whole class — you will inevitably 'differentiate by task', choosing levels of difficulty to suit everyone. As you see how the children respond you can then 'differentiate by outcome', adapting or extending the activity while the children are still engaged, or noting things to try on another occasion. The activities are sufficiently open in their design to allow for different development to suit different levels of attainment.

USING THE ACTIVITY PAGES

Children will experience

This section outlines what the children might be learning and hence indicates the main focus of assessment.

The name of the activity

The name of the activity is at the top of the left-hand page.

Equipment

This section lists what materials you will need to have available.

Getting started

This section provides an outline of an activity which can be adapted to several different levels of difficulty. It is a good idea to read this section in conjunction with the 'Can the children . . .' boxes. The suggestions in these boxes offer a guide to what children working at different levels can be expected to achieve in this area, and can help you both to initiate and to continue the activity at appropriate levels.

Section of book

We wanted to make clear the way in which this book corresponds with the sub-division of number and algebra in the national curriculum. To do this, we have grouped the ten parts of the book under three main headings: Place Value and Extending the Number System; Number Relationships and Operations; and Solving Numerical Problems. At the foot of every activity page (left and right) is a reminder about which of these three sections the activity is in.

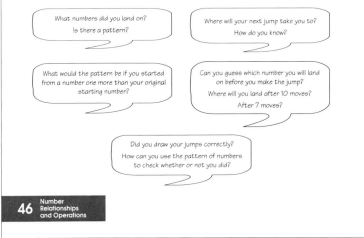

JUMP FROM WHERE?

Children will experience
- looking for number patterns
- predicting numbers using their knowledge of number patterns
- practice in using a number line

Equipment
- 0-100 number line
- decimal number line
- blank number line
- felt-tipped pens
- two dice
- pencil and paper

Getting started

You can introduce this activity to a group then split the children up into pairs.
- One child tosses a dice to find where to start on the line, and rings that number (with younger children you may want them to omit this, and start all their jump series from 0)
- The other child tosses both dice and adds the numbers together (or subtracts) to find the size of jump to draw
- The children then work together to draw jumps of this size from their starting-point, until they can go no further
- They should record on a piece of paper the numbers where they land

Older or more able children could explore jumping on a decimal number line, or a line showing both positive and negative numbers.

Questions to ask the children

> What numbers did you land on?
> Is there a pattern?

> Where will your next jump take you to?
> How do you know?

> What would the pattern be if you started from a number one more than your original starting number?

> Can you guess which number you will land on before you make the jump?
> Where will you land after 10 moves?
> After 7 moves?

> Did you draw your jumps correctly?
> How can you use the pattern of numbers to check whether or not you did?

46 Number Relationships and Operations

Questions to ask the children

These questions can help focus the children's attention on the mathematics and offer you valuable opportunities for assessment.

Ten parts, six tools

The activities in the book are divided into ten sections. At the top of the right-hand page there is a reminder of which of these the activity belongs in. Next comes which of the six tools the activity primarily focuses on (for an explanation of the 'six tools' see page *ii* of the Introduction).

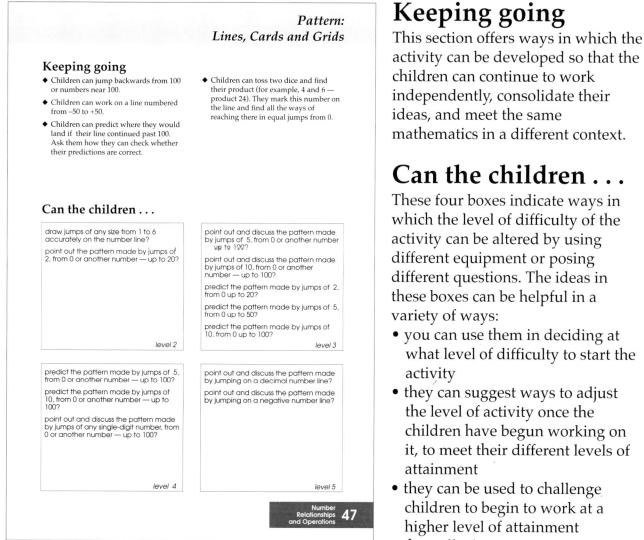

Pattern:
Lines, Cards and Grids

Keeping going

♦ Children can jump backwards from 100 or numbers near 100.

♦ Children can work on a line numbered from −50 to +50.

♦ Children can predict where they would land if their line continued past 100. Ask them how they can check whether their predictions are correct.

♦ Children can toss two dice and find their product (for example, 4 and 6 — product 24). They mark this number on the line and find all the ways of reaching there in equal jumps from 0.

Can the children . . .

| |
| draw jumps of any size from 1 to 6 accurately on the number line? |
| point out the pattern made by jumps of 2, from 0 or another number — up to 20? |
| *level 2* |

| |
| point out and discuss the pattern made by jumps of 5, from 0 or another number up to 100? |
| point out and discuss the pattern made by jumps of 10, from 0 or another number — up to 100? |
| predict the pattern made by jumps of 2, from 0 up to 20? |
| predict the pattern made by jumps of 5, from 0 up to 50? |
| predict the pattern made by jumps of 10, from 0 up to 100? |
| *level 3* |

| |
| predict the pattern made by jumps of 5, from 0 or another number — up to 100? |
| predict the pattern made by jumps of 10, from 0 or another number — up to 100? |
| point out and discuss the pattern made by jumps of any single-digit number, from 0 or another number — up to 100? |
| *level 4* |

| |
| point out and discuss the pattern made by jumping on a decimal number line? |
| point out and discuss the pattern made by jumping on a negative number line? |
| *level 5* |

Number Relationships and Operations **47**

Keeping going

This section offers ways in which the activity can be developed so that the children can continue to work independently, consolidate their ideas, and meet the same mathematics in a different context.

Can the children . . .

These four boxes indicate ways in which the level of difficulty of the activity can be altered by using different equipment or posing different questions. The ideas in these boxes can be helpful in a variety of ways:

• you can use them in deciding at what level of difficulty to start the activity

• they can suggest ways to adjust the level of activity once the children have begun working on it, to meet their different levels of attainment

• they can be used to challenge children to begin to work at a higher level of attainment

• they offer key questions to use in assessing the level of attainment at which individual children are working

Place Value and Extending the Number System

Reading, Writing and Ordering Numbers

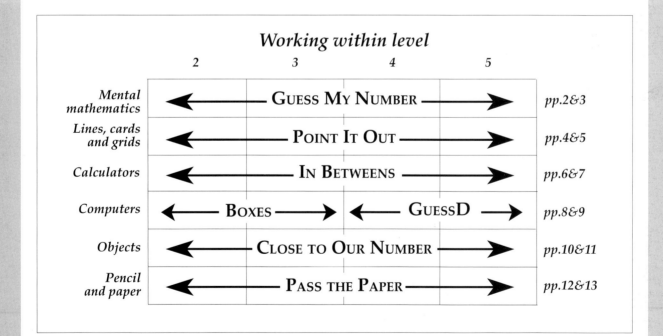

	Working within level				
	2	3	4	5	
Mental mathematics	←	GUESS MY NUMBER		→	pp.2&3
Lines, cards and grids	←	POINT IT OUT		→	pp.4&5
Calculators	←	IN BETWEENS		→	pp.6&7
Computers	← BOXES →		← GUESSD →		pp.8&9
Objects	←	CLOSE TO OUR NUMBER		→	pp.10&11
Pencil and paper	←	PASS THE PAPER		→	pp.12&13

GUESS MY NUMBER

Children will experience
◆ logical thinking
◆ thinking about and using the properties of numbers
◆ using place value and the size of numbers
◆ exploring and developing strategies

Equipment
◆ large sheets of paper and thick felt pens.
◆ number lines
◆ number squares
◆ software: 'Guess' in *The First 31* from SMILE

Getting started
This activity can be done in groups, or with the whole class.

Choose a number and give a clue about it e.g. "I'm thinking of a number between 0 and 10", or "I'm thinking of a number bigger than 20". Children ask questions to try and discover what number you have chosen. They may find it useful to cross out eliminated numbers on a number line or square.

Once they are familiar with the activity they can take turns to choose a number for the others to guess.

Important mathematics to discuss
You may want to limit the number of times children can ask "Is it more than . . ." (or less than) as they might otherwise use only that strategy.

Questions to ask the children

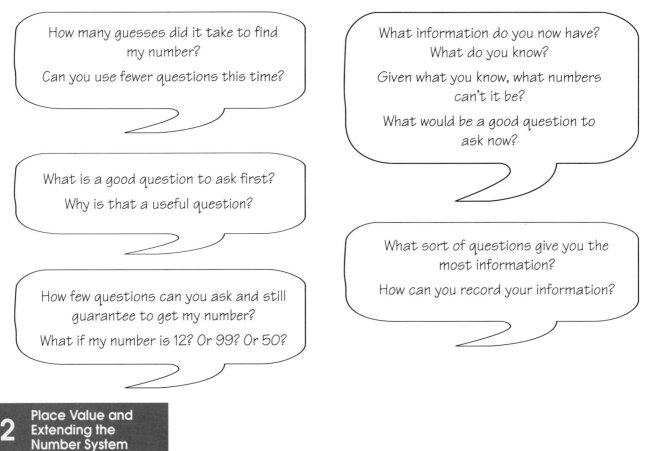

How many guesses did it take to find my number?

Can you use fewer questions this time?

What is a good question to ask first?

Why is that a useful question?

How few questions can you ask and still guarantee to get my number?

What if my number is 12? Or 99? Or 50?

What information do you now have? What do you know?

Given what you know, what numbers can't it be?

What would be a good question to ask now?

What sort of questions give you the most information?

How can you record your information?

Keeping going

◆ Children can record their questions and order them according to the amount of information they provide.

◆ Children can play 'Guess' on the computer.

◆ Children take turns to think of a secret number and challenge others to guess — only ten (or twenty) questions allowed.

◆ Children decide on their own secret number, then write down a series of facts about it which identify it and it alone.

Can the children . . .

ask questions to help them find numbers between 0 and at least 100?

describe numbers between 0 and at least 100 without naming the number?

give and use information such as 'It's odd' or 'It's a tens number' to help identify a number?

identify a number that is more/less than 50, 78 . . ?

level 2

---

ask questions to help them find numbers between 0 and at least 1000?

discuss which strategies are the most efficient for finding a number?

describe numbers between 0 and at least 1000 without naming the number?

give and use information such as 'it's odd and over 50' or 'it's a multiple of five' to identify a number?

identify a number that is more/less than 253, 579, 999 . . ?

level 3

---

develop and use strategies to predict numbers up to and beyond 1000?

develop and use strategies to predict numbers with simple fractional parts, for example $4^1/_2$?

be systematic in eliminating possible numbers?

identify a number that is more/less than 1000?

level 4

---

develop and use strategies to predict negative numbers and decimal numbers?

be systematic in eliminating possible numbers?

investigate the minimum number of questions needed to be certain of finding numbers between 0 and 100?

level 5

POINT IT OUT

Children will experience

- exploring place value and the size of numbers
- understanding that the place of a digit indicates its value
- familiarity with decimal numbers
- mental calculation

Equipment

- board / poster / flipchart / OHP / chalkboard / large piece of paper showing the following grid

1000	2000	3000	4000	5000	6000	7000	8000	9000
100	200	300	400	500	600	700	800	900
10	20	30	40	50	60	70	80	90
1	2	3	4	5	6	7	8	9
0.1	0.2	0.3	0.4	0.5	0.6	0.7	0.8	0.9
0.01	0.02	0.03	0.04	0.05	0.06	0.07	0.08	0.09

(Adjust the grid to a level appropriate to the children)

Getting started

This is a whole class or group activity. Point in turn to a number in each row, and ask children to read the whole number. For example, when you point to 1000, 200, 40, 3, 0.1, the children should say 'One thousand two hundred and forty three point one'.

You can use variations of this such as:

— pointing to the smallest number first
— pointing to numbers in any order
— pointing out numbers where there is a 0 in one place, such as 3056

Questions to ask the children

Can you point out 326? 4001?

Can you point out a number that is 10 times bigger than 25?
One that is 10 times smaller than 340?

Here is a number written down. Can you point it out?
Can you write down a number for someone else to point out?

Can you point out a number that is 10 more than 245?
10 less? 100 more? 100 less?

I am pointing out this number. Can you write it down?

Keeping going

◆ Children can make their own versions of the chart for work in pairs or small groups. When they do this activity with each other, get the 'pointer' to write down their number before pointing, lest they forget what it was.

◆ As an alternative to pointing, put counters on the numbers on the chart.

◆ Two children can point out a number each. Which is largest/smallest? Which is nearest 500?

◆ Point out a number. Is it odd or even? Can children round it to the nearest 10? To the nearest 100?

◆ Simplify the board for younger children.

◆ Extend the board to include the multiples of 1000, 10,000 and 100,000 and/or the multiples of 0.1, 0.01, 0.001.

◆ Use the board to play Roll a Penny.

Can the children . . .

point out numbers to at least 100?

read numbers to at least 100?

record numbers to at least 100?

add a multiple of 10 to any single-digit number?

level 2

point out numbers to at least 1000?

read numbers to at least 1000?

record numbers to at least 1000?

multiply any whole number by 10 mentally?

round any number to the nearest 10 or 100?

level 3

point out, read and record any whole number?

point out, read and record numbers with up to two places of decimals?

add or subtract any two two-digit numbers mentally?

divide any given number by 10 mentally?

multiply any given number by 10 or 100 mentally?

round any number to the nearest whole number?

level 4

point out, read and record numbers with more than two places of decimals?

add or subtract any two three-digit numbers mentally?

multiply any given number by any powers of ten mentally?

divide any given number by any powers of ten mentally?

round any number to any significant figure (including decimal places)?

level 5

IN BETWEENS

Children will experience

◆ logical thinking
◆ using place value and the size of numbers
◆ mental calculation

Equipment

◆ calculator for each child
◆ blank number line, with 10 intervals (this can be drawn on flipchart, OHP or chalkboard)

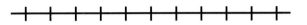

Getting started

This activity can be done with the whole class, but the children should be organised in groups of six. Write a number at each end of the number line and ask the children to use their calculators to find the number that belongs at the centre.

The children in each group should compare the numbers showing on their calculators with one another, then report back to the whole class.

Later, children can try this activity without using calculators.

Questions to ask the children

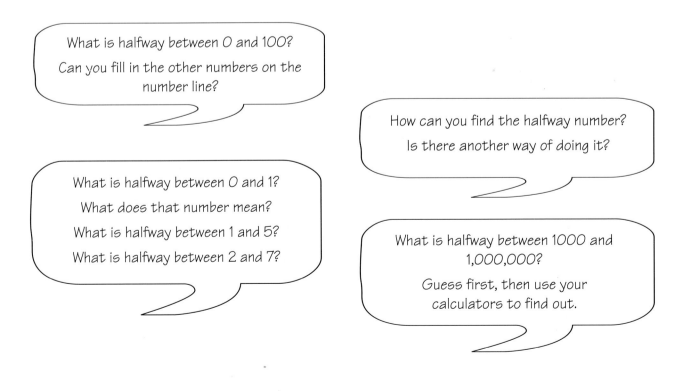

What is halfway between 0 and 100?
Can you fill in the other numbers on the number line?

How can you find the halfway number?
Is there another way of doing it?

What is halfway between 0 and 1?
What does that number mean?
What is halfway between 1 and 5?
What is halfway between 2 and 7?

What is halfway between 1000 and 1,000,000?
Guess first, then use your calculators to find out.

Keeping going

◆ Children use a blank number line with ten intervals to make up problems for each other such as 'The first number is 2, the third number 10. Fill in the other numbers.'

Children can work in pairs, creating ten problems to swap with each other.

◆ Children make up 'jumping' problems for each other such as 'My end number is 20, my middle number is 16. What number did I start at? What size were the jumps?'

◆ Children choose a starting number (such as 10) and a size of interval (such as 0.2) then fill in the numbers on the line accordingly. (To help them, they could use the constant function on a calculator.)

◆ Use a numbered line 0-20 and pick out number 16. Ask children what the value would be at that position if the scale went from 0-200 instead of 0-20?

Can the children . . .

estimate the halfway number for any two numbers under 100?

without the use of a calculator, find the halfway number for any two numbers under 100?

level 2

without the use of a calculator, find the halfway number for any two numbers under 1000, where the intervals on the number line are worth 1?

without the use of a calculator, find the halfway number for any two numbers under 1000, where the intervals on the number line are worth 10?

on a number line where the beginning and end numbers are under 1000, show approximately where any whole number belongs?

level 3

without the use of a calculator, find the halfway number for any two numbers under 1000, where the intervals on the number line are less than 10?

write in the numbers on a blank number line where the intervals are worth 1/10 or 1/100?

on a number line where the intervals are worth 1/10, give the approximate value of any point on the line?

level 4

without the use of a calculator, find the halfway number for any two numbers, including numbers to one or two decimal points? (for example, work out that 2.5 is halfway between 0.5 and 4)

on a line with beginning and end numbers to one or two decimal points, find the value for any marker — without the use of a calculator? (for example, on a ten-interval line from 0 to 5.5, work out that the first interval is 0.55)

level 5

BOXES AND GUESSD

Children will experience

◆ understanding that the place of a digit indicates its value

◆ familiarity with decimal numbers

Equipment

◆ software: 'Boxes 1', 'Boxes 2', 'Boxes 3', 'Boxes 5' (levels 2 and 3) in *Number Games* from LETSS

◆ software: 'GuessD' (levels 4 and 5) in *The First 31* from SMILE

Getting started

'Boxes 1' is a game for a pair or a small group, where the aim is to make three-, four-, or five-digit numbers, by placing digits in boxes. Children can play ten rounds and see who does best — they themselves or the computer.

'Boxes 2' is a game for pairs of children which gives them the opportunity to use and recognise the 'greater than' and 'less than' signs (> and <).

'Boxes 3' is a game for 2 players which helps children develop and practise place value and ordering skills. The aim of the game is to ensure that three numbers are in order.

'Boxes 5' is a game of strategy for 4 players which provides an opportunity to use and reinforce their understanding of place value.

'GuessD' is a game for pairs or small groups to practise ordering numbers.
The aim is to find an unknown decimal number between 1 and 10. The computer chooses a number, pupils try a number and are told whether it is too big or too small. At the end the computer shows how many guesses were required and how many were wasted.

Questions to ask the children

Where is the best place to put that digit?

Why is that a good place?

Could you have won the game if you had arranged the numbers differently?

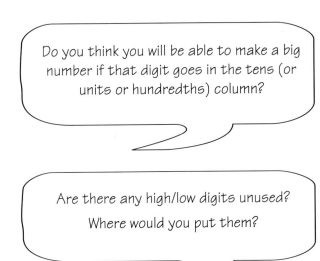

Do you think you will be able to make a big number if that digit goes in the tens (or units or hundredths) column?

Are there any high/low digits unused?

Where would you put them?

Keeping going

◆ Children can play the other Boxes games.

◆ Children can play 'Guess' which is similar to 'GuessD', but which involves whole numbers in the range 0-1000.

Can the children . . .

(Boxes 1, 2, 3, 5)

play the game successfully with two-digit numbers?

say the value of either digit in a two-digit number?

predict 'what would happen if' . . ?

put two-digit numbers in order?

level 2

(Boxes 1, 2, 3, 5)

say the value of either digit in a three-digit number?

use mental strategies to decide where to place digits?

explain why they put digits where they did?

develop strategies that maximise their chance of winning?

level 3

(GuessD)

read the numbers they make?

say which number is higher/lower?

use mental strategies to decide where to place digits?

develop strategies to guess the number in as few moves as possible?

develop the strategy of choosing the halfway mark?

level 4

(GuessD)

predict the minimum number of guesses required to get the chosen number?

make explicit the strategies they are using?

level 5

CLOSE TO OUR NUMBER

Children will experience

◆ using place value and the size of numbers
◆ understanding that the place of a digit indicates its value
◆ mental calculation
◆ exploring and developing strategies
◆ logical thinking

Equipment

◆ cubes or counters
◆ dice
◆ number cards 0-100 (or whatever numbers are appropriate)
◆ 'place value mat' for each player divided in three (or whatever is appropriate)

H	T	U

Getting started

This is a game for children to play in pairs. You can introduce it to a large group or the whole class and then split them up into pairs.

● Together they pick a number card to be the target number
● They then take turns to toss two (or three) dice and take that many cubes
● The children arrange their cubes on the mat to make a number as close as possible to the target; for example, a child aiming for 65 with nine cubes might put six in the tens place and three in the units place to make 63
● Each child writes down the number they have made; whoever's number is closer to the target is the winner
● The children keep a record of their score and continue until someone has scored ten points

Questions to ask the children

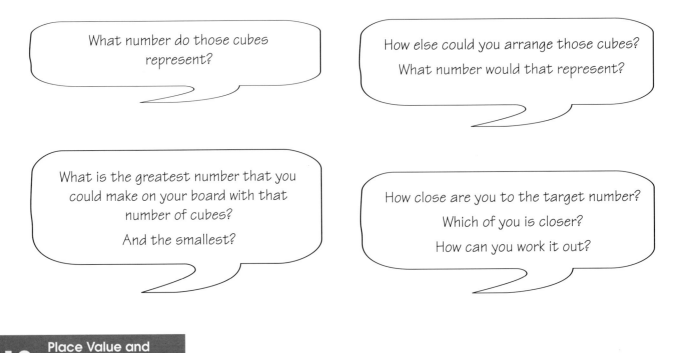

What number do those cubes represent?

How else could you arrange those cubes? What number would that represent?

What is the greatest number that you could make on your board with that number of cubes?

And the smallest?

How close are you to the target number?

Which of you is closer?

How can you work it out?

Keeping going

◆ Ask children to keep a record of the difference there is each time between their number and the target number. After ten goes, whoever has the lowest total of differences is the winner.

◆ Children can play with place value mats showing just tens and units; or showing thousands, hundreds, tens and units.

 Children can also use 'decimal' place value mats.

◆ Children could keep with the HTU mat but use different dice (say, 0-9 or 1-12) or three ordinary dice.

◆ Toss the dice, take that number of cubes, and investigate how many different numbers can be made with that number of cubes.

◆ Children can aim to make a number *as far away as possible* from the number on the card.

◆ Children can use a spike abacus instead of cubes and a place value mat.

Can the children . . .

play the game with two-digit numbers?

write two-digit numbers correctly?

read two-digit numbers correctly?

represent two-digit numbers correctly?

level 2

play the game with three-digit numbers?

write three-digit numbers correctly?

read three-digit numbers correctly?

represent three-digit numbers correctly?

level 3

play the game with numbers with two decimal places?

write numbers to two decimal places?

read numbers to two decimal places?

represent numbers to two decimal places?

level 4

play the game with numbers with three decimal places?

read decimal numbers to three decimal places?

write decimal numbers to three decimal places?

represent decimal numbers to three decimal places?

level 5

PASS THE PAPER

Children will experience

◆ familiarity with number patterns and sequences
◆ work on multiples
◆ mental calculation

Equipment

◆ paper for each player
◆ enough pens or pencils for each player, in a variety of colours
◆ an appropriately numbered number line may be useful

Getting started

This activity can be done with a group of any size.

Give each child a different coloured pen or pencil, if possible (to help you see afterwards who wrote which numbers). Agree on what the 'target number' is to be and the size of 'step'. (This needs to be determined by level. For example, a target of 100 and steps of five are suitable for level 2 . See *Can the children . . .* for information on other levels.)

Everyone writes down a number between 0 and 100. They pass their paper to the player on their left who writes down the next number in the series. For example, if the last number was 13 and the step is 'count back in 2s', they write down 11.

Children keep writing and passing the paper on until one person reaches, or passes, the target number.

Questions to ask the children

What number did the last person write? Was it correct? If not, quietly correct it.

What is a sensible target for steps of size 10 (or 2 or 0.5)?

What is a sensible size of step for a target of 400 (or 2 or –25)?

Look at the number you've just written. How many more people will write on it before it reaches or passes the target number?

Now we've finished, let's look at the papers.

Which starting numbers would have reached the target in the end? Which ones wouldn't ever reach it?

Why is that?

Keeping going

◆ A simpler version for a smallish group of younger children is to pass around just one piece of paper.

◆ Children can play this on their own in small groups. You can influence the choice of starting numbers, jump size and target numbers by providing number cards for children to pick from (use different colours of card for each set of numbers).

◆ Children can record the jumps on a number line. Another group can then try to work out what their rule was.

Can the children . . .

play Pass the Paper going forwards to a target of 100 using steps of 1 or 2?

play Pass the Paper going back to a target of 0 using steps of 1 or 2?

level 2

play Pass the Paper going forwards towards a target of 500 using steps of 2, 5 or 10?

play Pass the Paper going back from a number in the hundreds to a target of 0 using steps of 2, 5 or 10?

play Pass the Paper going back from 0 using steps of – 1 or –2?

level 3

play *Pass the* Paper going forwards and backwards using steps of any single-digit number?

play Pass the Paper going back from 0 using steps of – 5 or –10?

play Pass the Paper going forwards and backwards using steps of 0.1 or 0.2 or 0.5?

level 4

play *Pass the Paper* going forwards and backwards using steps of any two-digit number?

play Pass the Paper going back from 0 using steps of any single-digit number?

play Pass the Paper going forwards and backwards using steps of any size from 0.1 to 0.9?

level 5

Place Value and Extending the Number System

Decimals

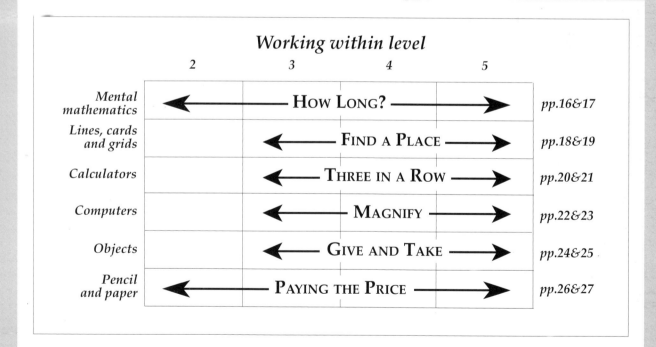

	Working within level			
	2	3	4	5
Mental mathematics	← —————	How Long?	————→	pp.16&17
Lines, cards and grids		← —	Find a Place —	→ pp.18&19
Calculators		← —	Three in a Row —	→ pp.20&21
Computers		← —	Magnify —	→ pp.22&23
Objects		←	Give and Take —	→ pp.24&25
Pencil and paper	← ———	Paying the Price	——→	pp.26&27

HOW LONG?

Children will experience
- familiarity with decimal numbers
- thinking about parts of a whole in terms of decimal numbers
- reading and writing measurements including use of the decimal point

Equipment
- metre stick
- decimetre measures (e.g card strip, 10-rod from Cuisenaire set, stick of 10 centicubes — all 10 cm long)
- paper and pencil

Getting Started

This activity starts with the whole class. The children suggest things in the classroom they think are longer/shorter than a metre. This list should be recorded on a flipchart or blackboard.

Children then get into groups of three. Each group, without moving from their seats, has to come to a group decision about each object's length in metres and decimetres (or, at level 2, metres and half metres). They record their suggestions in decimal notation. Then they can measure the objects and compare their measurements with their estimates.

Questions to ask the children

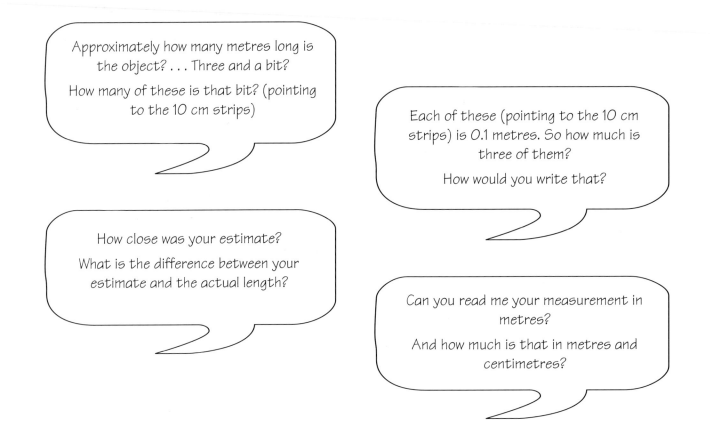

Approximately how many metres long is the object? . . . Three and a bit?

How many of these is that bit? (pointing to the 10 cm strips)

Each of these (pointing to the 10 cm strips) is 0.1 metres. So how much is three of them?

How would you write that?

How close was your estimate?

What is the difference between your estimate and the actual length?

Can you read me your measurement in metres?

And how much is that in metres and centimetres?

Keeping going

◆ Do the same activity, this time estimating whether various containers will hold more or less than 1 litre. Children should then go on to estimating the capacity using 100 ml measures.

◆ Do the same activity, with things that are heavier or lighter than 1 kg.

◆ Give children a bag of ribbons. Ask them to measure their lengths and write these in dm and cm.

Can the children . . .

record estimated lengths in metres and half metres using their own notation?
record measured lengths in metres and half metres using their own notation?
record estimated capacities in litres and half litres using their own notation?
record measured capacities in litres and half litres using their own notation?
level 2

estimate lengths/capacities/weights using whole units and 0.5 of a unit? (for example, say a weight is approximately 1.5 m or 2.5 kg)
record lengths/capacities/weights using whole units and 0.5 of a unit? (for example, write 1.5 m or 2.5 kg)
estimate lengths/capacities/weights to one place of decimals? (for example, say a length is approximately 2.3 m)
record lengths/capacities/weights to one place of decimals? (for example, write 2.3 m)   *level 3*

measure and record lengths/capacities/ weights to two place of decimals? (for example, 2.35 m or 5.72 kg)
level 4

convert one unit to another? (for example, say that 2.35 m is the same as 235 cm and 23.5 dm; write 5.72 kg as 5720 g)
level 5

FIND A PLACE

Children will experience

◆ reading and ordering whole and decimal numbers

◆ understanding that the place of a digit indicates its value

◆ familiarity with decimal numbers

◆ reasoning

Equipment

◆ pack of cards made up of one or two sets of cards with the digits 0-9 on them

◆ 'place value mat' for each player divided in three and showing tens, ones and tenths

tens	ones	tenths

Getting started

This is a game which works well with two or three players. You can introduce it to a group or the whole class before splitting the children up into twos and threes.

● Each player has a place value mat with an appropriate number of columns

● They shuffle the pack of cards and place them face down

● Players take it in turns to turn over the top card and place it in one of the columns on their mat

● They continue taking cards until everyone's mat is filled (or until a winner is clear)

● The winner is the person to make the highest number

Questions to ask the children

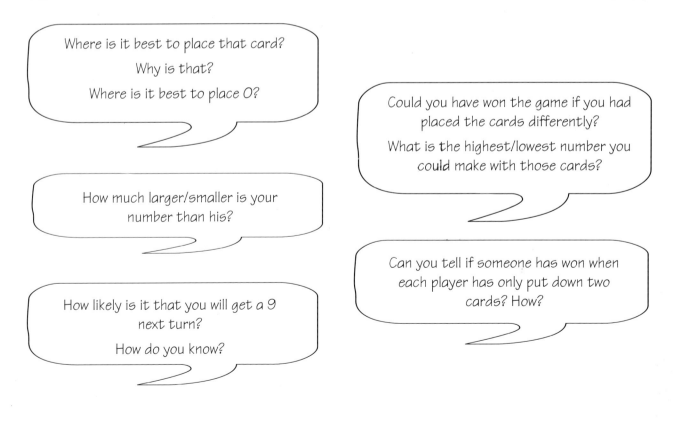

Where is it best to place that card?

Why is that?

Where is it best to place 0?

Could you have won the game if you had placed the cards differently?

What is the highest/lowest number you could make with those cards?

How much larger/smaller is your number than his?

Can you tell if someone has won when each player has only put down two cards? How?

How likely is it that you will get a 9 next turn?

How do you know?

Keeping going

◆ Adapt the place value mats to make the game easier or harder as necessary. An easier version has just ones and tenths. A harder has hundreds, tens, ones, tenths and hundredths!

◆ The winner is the person with the smallest number, the number nearest to 200, the biggest even number . . .

◆ A 'mean' version: cards can be placed on your own *or* your opponent's board — as a 'blocking' strategy.

◆ A solo activity: shuffle the cards and turn over three of them. Use these to make as many different three-digit numbers as possible. Record them in order, smallest to largest.

This activity can be adjusted according to children's level of attainment by using two, four or more cards, and asking them to make numbers with up to two decimal places.

Can the children . . .

<table>
<tr>
<td>

not appropriate

level 2
</td>
<td>

play the game successfully with tens, ones and tenths?

read the numbers they make?

say which of two numbers is higher?

develop strategies that maximise their chance of winning?

level 3
</td>
</tr>
<tr>
<td>

play the game using decimal numbers to two places of decimals?

read the numbers they make?

say which of two numbers is higher?

develop strategies that maximise their chance of winning in the 'mean' version of the game?

predict who is going to win?

level 4
</td>
<td>

play the game using decimal numbers to three or more places of decimals?

play the game with negative numbers?

read the numbers they make?

say which of two numbers is higher?

explain their winning strategies?

develop strategies that take into account which cards have already been used?

explain how they know when someone has definitely won — before the game is over?

level 5
</td>
</tr>
</table>

THREE IN A ROW

Children will experience

◆ ordering whole and decimal numbers

◆ writing decimal numbers

◆ logical thinking and planning

Equipment

◆ calculators

◆ $^1/_2$ cm squared paper

◆ a 0-5 number line marked in intervals of 0.5 (0, 0.5, 1, 1.5, 2, 2.5, . . .)

◆ three 0-9 dice or spinners

◆ pens or pencils in two colours

Getting started

This is a game for two children, each with a different coloured pen, using a 0-5 number line marked in intervals of 0.5.

```
┼─┼─┼─┼─┼─┼─┼─┼─┼─┼─┼
0  0.5  1  1.5  2  2.5  3  3.5  4  4.5  5
```

● They take turns to toss two dice, choose one of the numbers, then use a calculator to divide it by two

● They mark that number on the line, with their coloured pen

● The first person to get three of their marks in a row is the winner

A harder version uses three dice, and a number line from 0 to 5 on $^1/_2$ cm squared paper, leaving 5 or 10 intervals between each number.

```
┼┼┼┼┼┼┼┼┼┼┼┼┼┼┼┼┼┼┼┼┼┼┼┼┼┼
0        1        2        3        4        5
```

● The first player tosses the dice and chooses two of them to make into a 'division sum', dividing one number by the other with the help of a calculator (for example, given a throw of 9, 7 and 5, the player chooses to do 9 ÷ 7 and rounds the answer to 1.3)

● She marks this number on the line with a coloured pen

● The next player now does the same thing

● The first person to get three of their marks in a row is the winner

Questions to ask the children

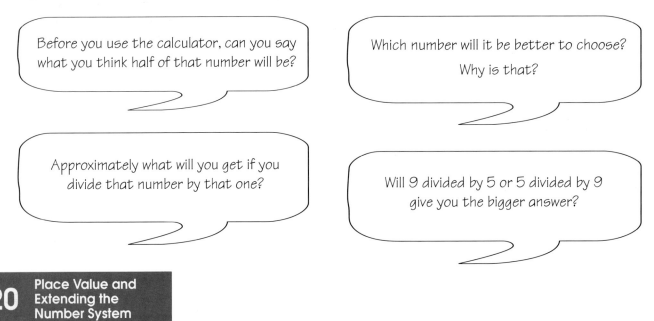

Before you use the calculator, can you say what you think half of that number will be?

Which number will it be better to choose? Why is that?

Approximately what will you get if you divide that number by that one?

Will 9 divided by 5 or 5 divided by 9 give you the bigger answer?

Keeping going

◆ Always divide the chosen number by three or four instead of two. (You may choose to provide an appropriately numbered line, or encourage children to work out for themselves where their numbers fit on the basic line.)

◆ Use a third dice in a different colour showing only 2 and 4. Children choose their number as usual, and the 2s/4s dice tells them whether to divide by 2 or by 4.

Can the children . . .

not appropriate
level 2

play the simpler version of the game without assistance?

divide a number by two on the calculator and read the answer?

make a good attempt at predicting the result of dividing a number by two on the calculator?

find the number on the line which matches the number in the calculator display?

level 3

when playing the simpler version of the game, predict the result of dividing a number by two on the calculator?

play the harder version of the game without assistance?

say approximately what will be the result of dividing a number by another one on the calculator?

round decimal numbers shown in the calculator display up or down to the nearest tenth?

find the appropriate place on the number line for their numbers?

level 4

sometimes be accurate in predicting the result of multiplying a number by another one on the calculator?

level 5

Magnify

Children will experience

◆ writing decimal numbers
◆ using trial and improvement methods to find a specific number
◆ working with decimal numbers

Equipment

◆ software: 'Magnify' in *11 More* from SMILE

Getting started

'Magnify' is a game that can be played by two pupils against one another or against the computer. It provides practice in ordering and writing numbers with up to three decimal places.

● The computer shows a segment of number line with a red marker on it which represents a decimal number

● Children type in two numbers, one which they think is less than (or equal to) the marker and one that they think is more than (or equal to) it

● If either of the numbers is exactly on the marker the game finishes

● If the decimal number is not yet found, the scale then expands so that the numbers typed in become the new end points, thus narrowing down the range of numbers

Questions to ask the children

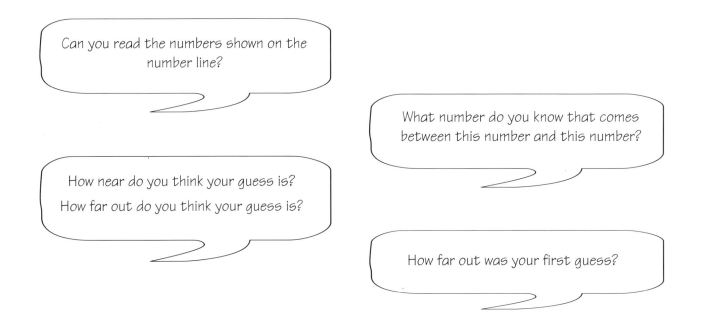

Can you read the numbers shown on the number line?

What number do you know that comes between this number and this number?

How near do you think your guess is?
How far out do you think your guess is?

How far out was your first guess?

Keeping going

◆ Children can play 'GuessD' which is a game for pairs or small groups to practise ordering numbers. The aim is to find an unknown decimal number between 1 and 10.

The computer chooses a number, children try a number, and are told whether it is too big or too small. At the end the computer shows how many guesses were required and how many were wasted.

◆ Children can play 'Tenners' (from SMILE's *11 More*). The activity, for pairs or small groups, explores place value including numbers with up to three decimal places.

A chart appears on screen with four different numbers. Children multiply or divide them by 10, 100 or 1000 to make them identical in as few moves as possible.

Can the children . . .

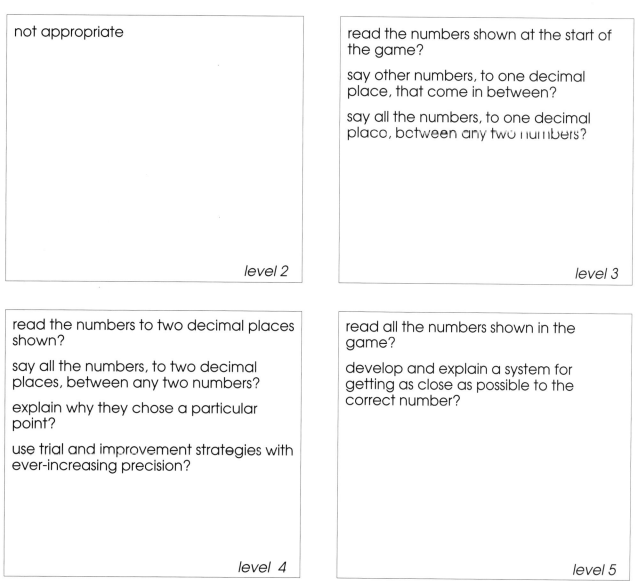

not appropriate

level 2

read the numbers shown at the start of the game?

say other numbers, to one decimal place, that come in between?

say all the numbers, to one decimal place, between any two numbers?

level 3

read the numbers to two decimal places shown?

say all the numbers, to two decimal places, between any two numbers?

explain why they chose a particular point?

use trial and improvement strategies with ever-increasing precision?

level 4

read all the numbers shown in the game?

develop and explain a system for getting as close as possible to the correct number?

level 5

GIVE AND TAKE

Children will experience

◆ familiarity with decimal numbers
◆ dividing pairs of numbers which result in decimal numbers
◆ logical thinking and planning

Equipment

◆ counters
◆ calculators
◆ two ordinary dice (numbered 1 to 6)
◆ blank dice
◆ dice showing g, g, g, t, t, t ('g' stands for 'give' and 't' for 'take')

Getting started

This is a game for a pair of children, each with 10 counters, and sharing the two ordinary dice and the give-and-take dice. You can introduce it to a group or the whole class before splitting the children up into pairs.

● The first player tosses all three dice
● They then use the two dice-numbers to make a 'division sum'; the child can choose which way round it is (for example, with 4 and 6 the sum could be 4 ÷ 6 or 6 ÷ 4)
● They work out the answer and round it up or down to the nearest whole number
● They then give that number of counters to, or take them from, the other player, depending on how the give-and-take dice landed
● Both players continue taking turns like this until one child has won all the counters from the other

Questions to ask the children

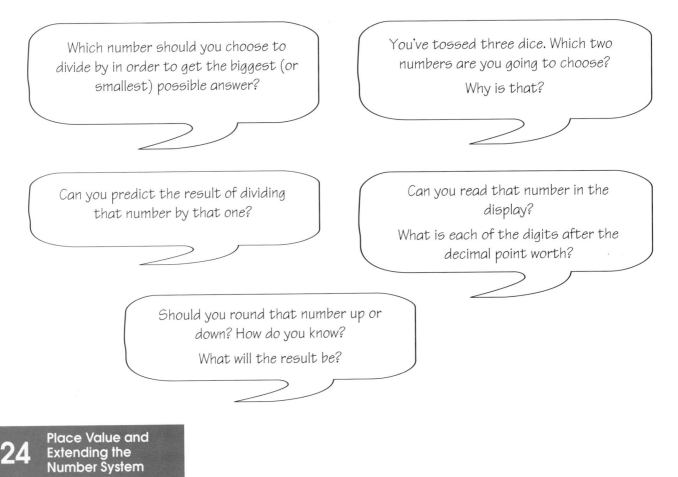

Which number should you choose to divide by in order to get the biggest (or smallest) possible answer?

You've tossed three dice. Which two numbers are you going to choose?

Why is that?

Can you predict the result of dividing that number by that one?

Can you read that number in the display?

What is each of the digits after the decimal point worth?

Should you round that number up or down? How do you know?

What will the result be?

Keeping going

◆ Children could use three numbered dice and choose which two to use each time.

◆ At a more advanced level, children can use base ten blocks (just 'longs' worth one and 'singles' worth 0.1) instead of counters. They could also use dice showing higher numbers. Children play as before, but rounding the numbers to the nearest tenth. They give their partner (or take from them) base ten blocks accordingly.

Can the children . . .

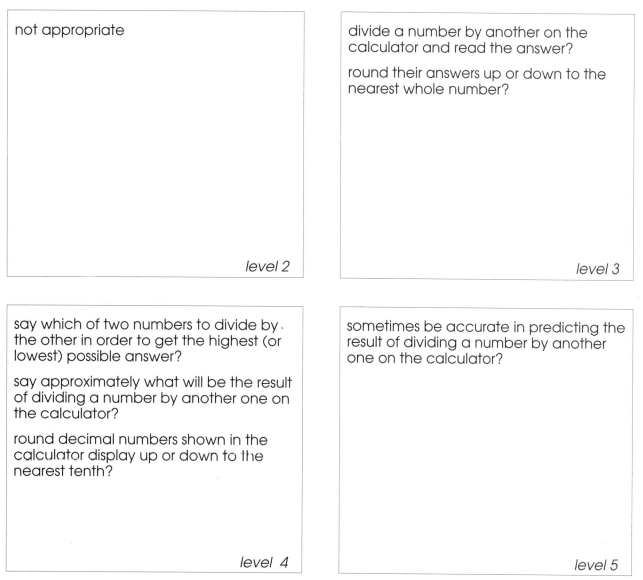

not appropriate

level 2

divide a number by another on the calculator and read the answer?

round their answers up or down to the nearest whole number?

level 3

say which of two numbers to divide by the other in order to get the highest (or lowest) possible answer?

say approximately what will be the result of dividing a number by another one on the calculator?

round decimal numbers shown in the calculator display up or down to the nearest tenth?

level 4

sometimes be accurate in predicting the result of dividing a number by another one on the calculator?

level 5

PAYING THE PRICE

Children will experience

◆ reading and writing sums of money including use of the decimal point
◆ calculating with money
◆ logical thinking and planning

Equipment

◆ supermarket bills
◆ catalogues
◆ coins
◆ calculators
◆ calculators which can do print-outs (optional)

Getting started

Lower levels

Children can work in pairs or groups. Give the children a supermarket bill or shopping catalogue and let everyone choose an item from it. Ask them what coins or notes they could use to pay for just that item — or for the whole bill. (If possible set the problem in a real context such as shopping for a class party, or buying food for the school rabbits.)

Higher levels

Give children a problem such as 'You have £50 to spend on your party, to which 11 people are coming. Decide how you will spend it.' (Again, if possible make the problem a real one, based on plans for a class outing, end of term party, school garden . . .)

Questions to ask the children

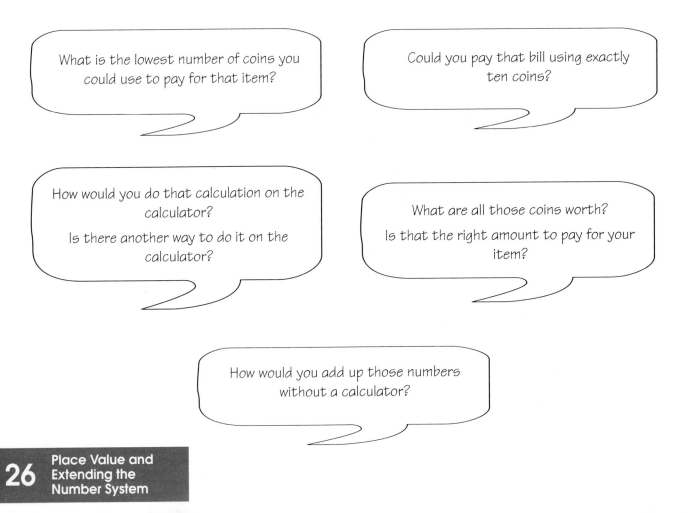

What is the lowest number of coins you could use to pay for that item?

Could you pay that bill using exactly ten coins?

How would you do that calculation on the calculator?

Is there another way to do it on the calculator?

What are all those coins worth?

Is that the right amount to pay for your item?

How would you add up those numbers without a calculator?

Keeping going

◆ *Levels 2 and 3*
Children could go on to make up their own supermarket bills.

◆ *Levels 4 and 5*
Children could use catalogues to plan how to spend a £500 windfall.

Can the children . . .

---

read out a sum of money correctly, such as £1.25?

write a sum of money correctly, such as £1.25?

find appropriate coins to pay for a sum ot money such as £1.25?

know the equivalent in pennies of a sum such as £1.25 (125p)?

level 2

---

use pencil and paper to work out what coins could be used to pay a sum of money such as £5.25?

use pencil and paper to work out the fewest coins that could be used to pay a sum of money such as £5.25?

level 3

---

work out mentally what coins could be used to pay a sum of money such as £5.25?

work out mentally the fewest coins that could be used to pay a sum of money such as £5.25?

make detailed plans for how to spend £10.00?

level 4

---

make detailed plans for how to spend £100.00?

level 5

Fractions and Percentages

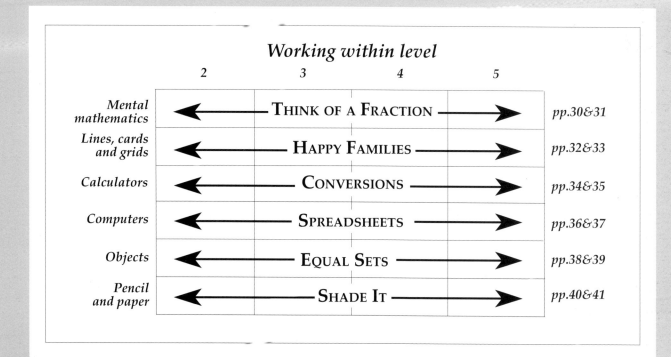

THINK OF A FRACTION

Children will experience

◆ working with fractions on a number line
◆ comparing the size of fractions
◆ devising questions about fractions
◆ developing a mental model of fractions in order

Equipment

◆ fraction number lines marked up in appropriate intervals for the denominator you are using

```
+----+----+----+----+----+----+----+----+----+----+----+----+----+----+----+----+----+----+----+----+
0   1/5  2/5  3/5  4/5  1  1 1/5 1 2/5 1 3/5 1 4/5 2  2 1/5 2 2/5 2 3/5 2 4/5 3  3 1/5 3 2/5 3 3/5 3 4/5 4
```

◆ number lines with unnumbered markers between the whole numbers

```
+--+--+--+--+--+--+--+--+--+--+--+--+--+--+--+--+--+--+--+--+
0           1           2           3           4
```

Getting started

You can do this with the whole class or a smaller group.

Decide on the denominator you want to use (say, 5) and have ready a number line marked to match — in this case in fifths.

In secret choose a number involving fractions such as $2^3/_5$. Say "I'm thinking of a number" and encourage children to guess what it is by asking questions. At first you might want to allow any questions, but later you can restrict them to questions with a 'yes' or 'no' answer.

When the children are familiar with the activity, they can take turns to choose a secret number.

Important mathematics to discuss

This activity leads to the idea of equivalent fractions, unless the denominator chosen is a prime number. If, for example, you are working in ninths a child may choose a secret number and describe it as three ninths. Accept this, but be prepared for a discussion about how it can also be described as one third.

Working at level 2 with a number line marked in quarters should lead to a discussion about how one half is the same as two quarters.

Questions to ask the children

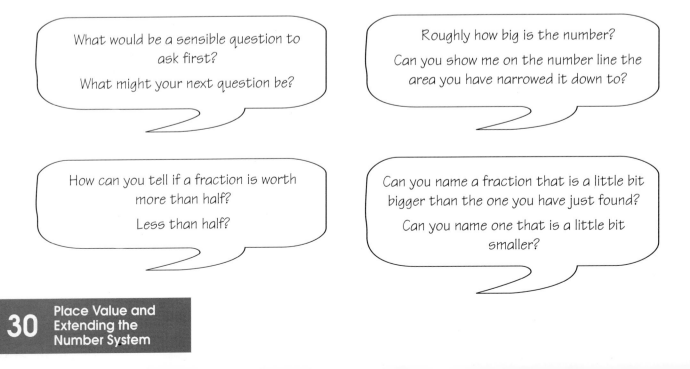

What would be a sensible question to ask first?

What might your next question be?

Roughly how big is the number?

Can you show me on the number line the area you have narrowed it down to?

How can you tell if a fraction is worth more than half?

Less than half?

Can you name a fraction that is a little bit bigger than the one you have just found?

Can you name one that is a little bit smaller?

Keeping going

◆ Tell the children the size of the denominator and use a number line with no markers between the whole numbers. Let the children find and mark the approximate position for the fraction.

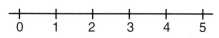

◆ Do the same activities using decimal numbers.

◆ Children can think up and record useful questions to ask next time they play.

◆ Children are only allowed ten questions to find the number.

Can the children . . .

ask sensible questions to discover secret numbers involving halves and quarters?

find numbers involving halves and quarters on the appropriate fraction line?

level 2

ask sensible questions to find secret numbers involving thirds, fifths, eighths and tenths?

find numbers involving these fractions on the appropriate fraction line?

level 3

ask sensible questions to discover secret numbers involving fractions with any denominator of 10 or less, and sixteenths? (for example, $^1/_8$, $^3/_7$, $1^1/_9$, or $^2/_{16}$)

find the approximate position for these on a number line with no markers between whole numbers?

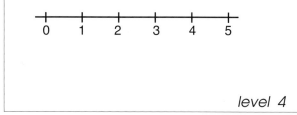

level 4

discover any fraction by asking questions?

devise a strategy for asking questions and describe it?

state the relative size of two fractions with different denominators?

find the approximate position for any fraction on a number line with no markers between whole numbers?

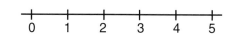

level 5

HAPPY FAMILIES

Children will experience

- working with fractions practically
- naming fractions
- reading and writing fraction notation
- reading and writing decimal notation
- reading and writing percentages notation
- thinking about equivalent fractions, decimals and percentages

Equipment

- blank cards
- pack of 30 cards showing ten numbers each represented as a fraction, a decimal and a percentage (for example, $1/2$, 0.5 and 50%)
- number line
- calculator

Getting started

These activities suit a group of up to four children.

Levels 2 & 3

Children work together and use the blank cards to make a set of cards showing shapes such as circles, squares, octagons and hexagons. The pack of cards should contain four of each shape: one with the whole shape coloured in, one with half coloured, one with a quarter, and one with three quarters.

The children use these cards to play Happy Families.

Levels 4 & 5

Ask the children to sort out the pack of prepared cards described in the 'Equipment' section above, putting together numbers of the same value (such as $1/5$, 0.2 and 20%). They can then shuffle the cards and use them to play Happy Families, Pelmanism or Snap.

Questions to ask the children

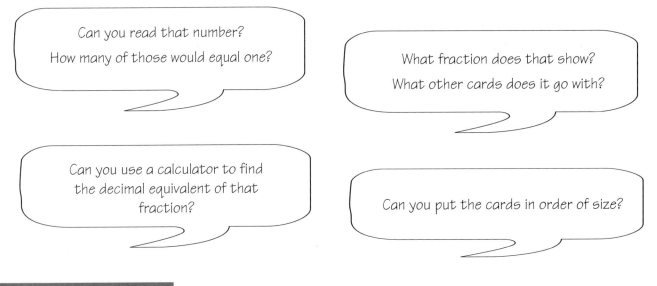

Can you read that number?
How many of those would equal one?

What fraction does that show?
What other cards does it go with?

Can you use a calculator to find the decimal equivalent of that fraction?

Can you put the cards in order of size?

Keeping going

◆ Children can add to the set of shape cards using, for example, thirds and fifths.

◆ Make a pack of 20 cards showing ten numbers represented as a fraction and pictorially (for instance, by shading part of the card). Children can use these to play Happy Families or Pelmanism.

◆ Children working at the higher levels can add a new mini-set to the pack of prepared cards — for example, $1/20$, 0.05 and 5%. Or they could enlarge the mini-sets by adding some equivalent fractions — for example, the set of cards $1/2$, 0.5 and 50% could be enlarged by the addition of $2/4$, $5/10$, and $10/20$.

Can the children . . .

recognise and name a half, a quarter and three quarters of whole objects?

level 2

read and write the fractions $1/2, 1/4$, and $3/4$?

read simple fractions such as $2/3$ and $1/5$?

level 3

match a variety of simple written fractions, percentages and decimals? (for example, say that these cards show equivalent numbers)

0.2 $1/5$ 20%

level 4

match increasingly complex written fractions, percentages and decimals, using a calculator where appropriate? (for example, say that these cards show equivalent numbers)

0.05 $5/100$ 5% $1/20$

level 5

CONVERSIONS

Children will experience

◆ reading and writing fraction and decimal notation

◆ exploring equivalent fractions and decimals

◆ refining estimations

Equipment

◆ calculators

◆ Galaxy 9x calculators or other calculators that convert fractions to decimals and vice versa

Getting started

This activity can be done with the whole class or a group of any size. Ask children to work in pairs. One child writes down a fraction, and they both estimate what size of decimal number it will be when converted on the calculator. They then test this out by doing the division.

(The Galaxy 9x is an excellent calculator to use as it allows children to display a number as a vulgar fraction and then converts it to a decimal — and back again if desired — at the press of a button.)

$\frac{1}{4}$

It will be about 0.2
We pressed 1 ÷ 4 =

It was 0.25

Questions to ask the children

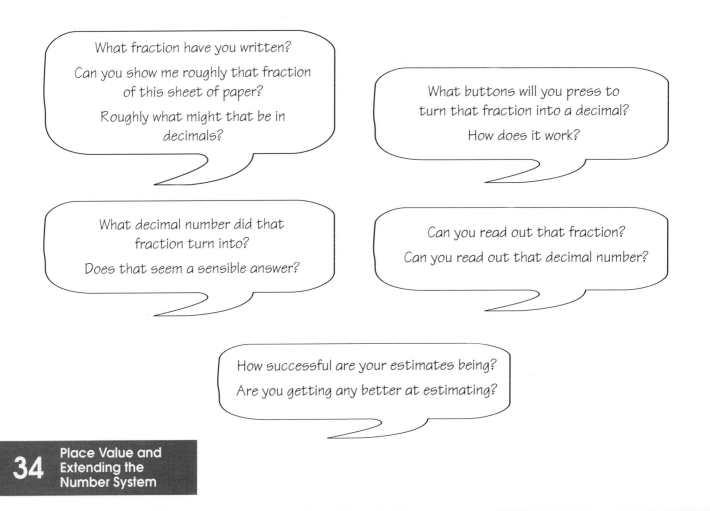

What fraction have you written?

Can you show me roughly that fraction of this sheet of paper?

Roughly what might that be in decimals?

What buttons will you press to turn that fraction into a decimal?

How does it work?

What decimal number did that fraction turn into?

Does that seem a sensible answer?

Can you read out that fraction?

Can you read out that decimal number?

How successful are your estimates being?

Are you getting any better at estimating?

Keeping going

◆ Children can work converting fractions
  and decimals into percentages — or the
  other way round.

◆ A pair of children can record their work
  for another pair, including a deliberate
  mistake. The challenge is to spot the
  deliberate mistake.

Can the children . . .

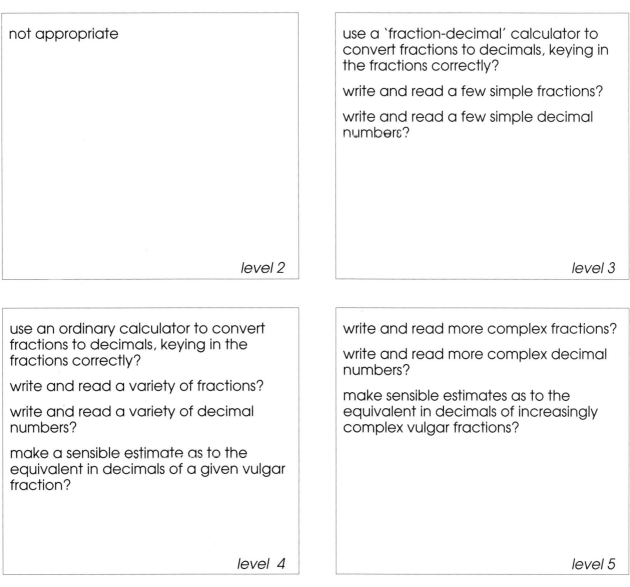

not appropriate	use a 'fraction-decimal' calculator to convert fractions to decimals, keying in the fractions correctly?
	write and read a few simple fractions?
	write and read a few simple decimal numbers?
level 2	*level 3*
use an ordinary calculator to convert fractions to decimals, keying in the fractions correctly?	write and read more complex fractions?
write and read a variety of fractions?	write and read more complex decimal numbers?
write and read a variety of decimal numbers?	make sensible estimates as to the equivalent in decimals of increasingly complex vulgar fractions?
make a sensible estimate as to the equivalent in decimals of a given vulgar fraction?	
level 4	*level 5*

SPREADSHEETS

Children will experience

◆ predicting numbers in a pattern

◆ operating with division, giving rise to decimals

◆ exploring the relationship between fractions and decimals

Equipment

◆ any spreadsheet program

Getting started

This activity can be done with a small group of children. It is fairly easy and can be used to introduce spreadsheets to children who have not used them before. When they are confident, each child in the original group can take responsibility for teaching another child how to use a spreadsheet to explore the division of numbers.

Help children to enter numbers 1 to 10 in the first column. These are 'inputs'. The next column should divide each of the input numbers by 2, and the next column should divide them by 3. You can set the display to round up to two decimal places.

You will end up with a table like this:

Children can then go on to add further columns, exploring other divisions.

input	output1	output 2
1	0.5	0.33
2	1	0.67
3	1.5	1.00
4	2	1.33
5	2.5	1.67
6	3	2.00
7	3.5	2.33
8	4	2.67
9	4.5	3.00
10	5	3.33

Questions to ask the children

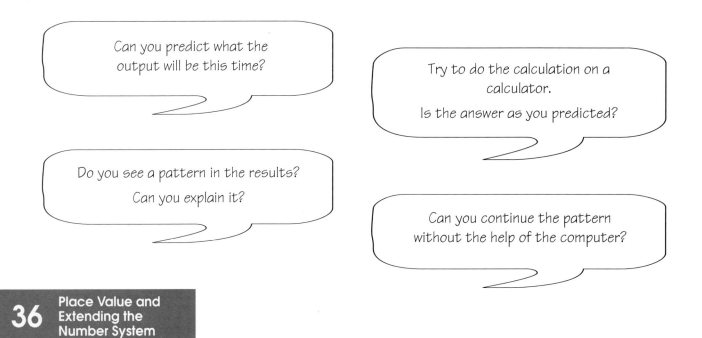

Can you predict what the output will be this time?

Try to do the calculation on a calculator.

Is the answer as you predicted?

Do you see a pattern in the results?

Can you explain it?

Can you continue the pattern without the help of the computer?

Keeping going

◆ Children can go on to explore other operations, and strings of operations, on a spreadsheet.

◆ One children 'teaches' the spreadsheet an operation in secret. Their partner inputs various numbers and tries to work out what the secret operation is.

◆ Children can display their outputs as percentages of the inputs by changing the way the numbers are formatted.

Can the children . . .

<table>
<tr>
<td>

not appropriate

level 2
</td>
<td>

explore $^1/_2$, $^1/_5$ and $^1/_{10}$ of numbers 1 to 10?

predict what $^1/_2$, $^1/_5$ and $^1/_{10}$ of any number up to 100 will be?

recognise 0.5 as $^1/_2$, 0.2 as $^1/_5$ and 0.1 us $^1/_{10}$?

level 3
</td>
</tr>
<tr>
<td>

explore $^1/_3$ and $^1/_4$ of numbers 1 to 10?

predict what $^1/_3$ and $^1/_4$ of any number up to 100 will be?

recognise 0.3333 as the decimal display of $^1/_3$?

recognise 0.25 as $^1/_4$?

level 4
</td>
<td>

explore other fractions of numbers 1 to 10?

predict what other fractions of any number up to 100 will be?

recognise various fractions written as decimals?

understand that decimal notation is an imprecise way of displaying some fractions?

level 5
</td>
</tr>
</table>

EQUAL SETS

Children will experience
◆ working with fractions practically
◆ naming fractions
◆ writing numbers using fraction notation
◆ exploring fractions of a number

Equipment
◆ conkers, counters, cubes, bottle tops . . .
◆ pencil and paper

Getting started

This is an activity for children working in pairs. You can introduce it to a group or the whole class before splitting the children into twos.

● The children each take a handful of counters (or conkers, cubes, bottle tops . . .) and combine them into one set
● They then work together to see how this set can be split up into equal sub-sets
● They record their division, using fractional language
● Then they recombine the set and see how else it can be split up into equal sub-sets

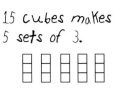

15 cubes makes 5 sets of 3.

Each set of 3 is 1/5 of the whole. 3 is 1/5 of 15.

Questions to ask the children

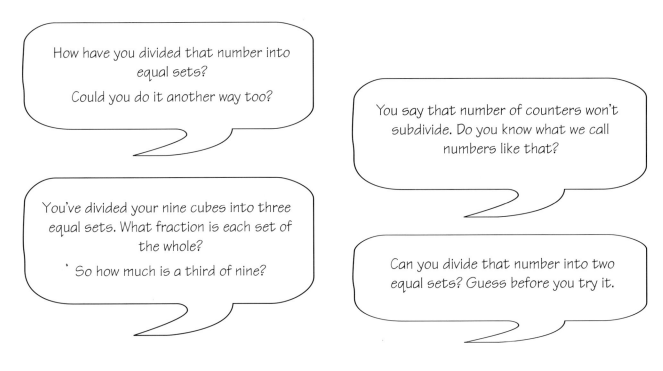

How have you divided that number into equal sets?

Could you do it another way too?

You say that number of counters won't subdivide. Do you know what we call numbers like that?

You've divided your nine cubes into three equal sets. What fraction is each set of the whole?

So how much is a third of nine?

Can you divide that number into two equal sets? Guess before you try it.

Keeping going

◆ Children can find or collect their own 'counters' to use for this activity — coloured pencils, toy cars, grapes, fir cones . . .

◆ Children can notice and discuss those numbers which sub-divide in lots of ways and those that don't sub-divide at all.

◆ *Frackers*

You need cards (some with 4 spots, some with 12, some with 12 and some with 16) and a dice marked with $^1/_2$, $^1/_2$, $^1/_4$, $^1/_4$, $^3/_4$, $^3/_4$.

Players take turns to toss the dice, turn up the top card and score the appropriate fraction — for example, if the dice shows $^1/_2$ and the card has 16 spots they score 8. Keep track of the scores to see who wins.

Can the children . . .

divide a set of counters into equal sub-sets and record their work using whole numbers? (for example, '12 is 3 sets of 4') *level 2*

divide a set of counters into equal sub-sets and record their work using fractional numbers? (for example, '4 is $^1/_3$ of 12') *level 3*

divide a set of counters into equal sub-sets and use this to make a range of statements about fractional numbers? (for example, '$^1/_3$ of 12 is 4 and $^2/_3$ of 12 is 8') *level 4*

divide a number into equal sub-sets, using only pencil and paper and calculators? record their work using fractional numbers? (for example, '$^1/_5$ of 70 is 14 and $^2/_5$ of 70 is 28') *level 5*

SHADE IT

Children will experience

- working with fractions and percentages practically
- naming fractions and percentages
- addition of fractions and percentages
- relationships between different fractions and percentages

Equipment

- A5 scrap paper
- 2 cm or 5 cm squared paper
- coloured pens or pencils

Getting started

This is an activity for groups or the whole class.

Children each need a sheet of paper which they should fold in half, then in half again and again, to produce eight segments. (With younger children you might want to stick to two folds, producing four segments). Alternatively children need eight (or four) squares worth of squared paper.

Ask them to colour $1/4$ of the sheet with one colour. Now ask them to colour in $2/_8$ of the sheet with another colour, and $3/_8$ of the sheet with yet another colour. Ask them how much of the sheet is left uncoloured.

Children should now take a new sheet of paper and fold it in some other way in order to colour in other (harder) fractions such as $1/_{16}$ or $1/_6$.

When children are familiar with the activity, they can fold their papers into ten segments and do the activity with percentages instead of fractions.

Questions to ask the children

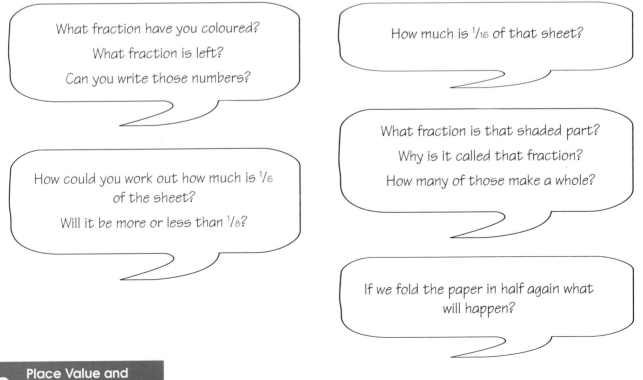

What fraction have you coloured?
What fraction is left?
Can you write those numbers?

How much is $1/_{16}$ of that sheet?

How could you work out how much is $1/_6$ of the sheet?
Will it be more or less than $1/_8$?

What fraction is that shaded part?
Why is it called that fraction?
How many of those make a whole?

If we fold the paper in half again what will happen?

Keeping going

◆ Children could make up addition 'sums' based on the sheets they have coloured.

$$1/8 + 7/8 = 8/8 = 1$$

◆ You or the children could invent a game using a fractions dice, based on colouring fractions of a sheet of paper.

◆ The ancient Egyptians only ever used fractions with 1 as the numerator ($1/2$, $1/8$, $1/3$, and so on). Ask children to fold a sheet of paper into twelve sections and see what different Egyptian fractions they can colour in. What about if they folded a sheet into eight, ten or sixteen segments?

Can the children . . .

identify and colour half of the piece of paper?

identify and colour $1/4$ and $3/4$ of the piece of paper?

level 2

identify and colour $1/8$, $3/8$ and $1/16$ of the piece of paper?

write the appropriate fractions on the areas coloured?

identify and colour 50%, 10% or 30% of the piece of paper?

write the appropriate percentages on the areas coloured?

level 3

use their work to identify and write simple fraction 'sums'? (for example, '$1/16$ and $1/16$ makes $1/8$')

identify percentage equivalents of fractions such as $1/2$ and $1/4$?

level 4

identify percentage equivalents of fractions such as $2/4$ and $1/8$?

level 5

Number Relationships and Operations

Pattern

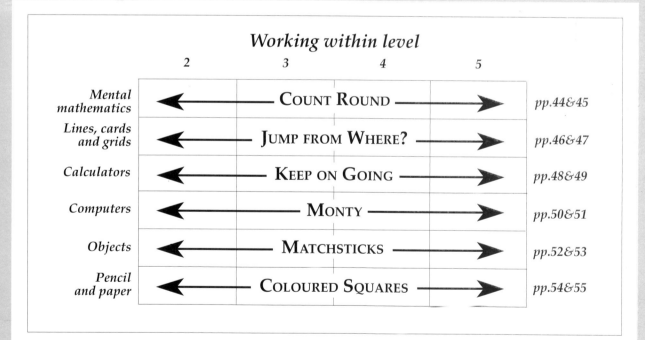

Working within level

	2	3	4	5	
Mental mathematics	←	COUNT ROUND		→	*pp.44&45*
Lines, cards and grids	←	JUMP FROM WHERE?		→	*pp.46&47*
Calculators	←	KEEP ON GOING		→	*pp.48&49*
Computers	←	MONTY		→	*pp.50&51*
Objects	←	MATCHSTICKS		→	*pp.52&53*
Pencil and paper	←	COLOURED SQUARES		→	*pp.54&55*

COUNT ROUND

Children will experience
◆ counting in number series
◆ looking for number patterns
◆ predicting numbers using their knowledge of number patterns

Equipment
◆ number line (optional)

Getting started

This activity can be done with a whole class. However, for assessment purposes it will be better to work with a smallish group.

Children sit in a circle and count round in ones, twos, fives, threes . . . , starting from 0, from 1 or from another number. (You might at this stage want to record the numbers in order to help children focus on the patterns rather than just saying the right number.)

When they have done this for a while ask them to continue as before, except that when it is their turn they should only say the units number. So for example, counting on in fives from 0 would go '5, 0, 5, 0, . . .'; counting on in threes from 0 would go '3, 6, 9, 2, 5, 8, 1, . . .'.

Questions to ask the children

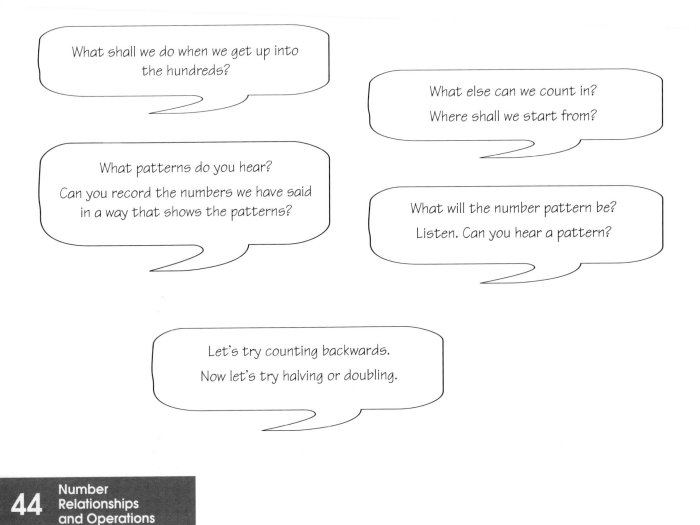

What shall we do when we get up into the hundreds?

What else can we count in?
Where shall we start from?

What patterns do you hear?
Can you record the numbers we have said in a way that shows the patterns?

What will the number pattern be?
Listen. Can you hear a pattern?

Let's try counting backwards.
Now let's try halving or doubling.

Keeping going

◆ Children can only say the tens number: counting in sevens from 0 would go '7, 1, 2, 2, 3, . . .'

◆ Children can work with decimals or vulgar fractions.

◆ A large group of children sit in a circle, saying the numbers in turn. Everybody who says the number five (or two, three, zero . . .) stands up. What is the pattern of standing-up sitting-down children?

◆ Children can try a different 'round' game: start with 56 (or some other number); the next person must give a divisor of that number, other than 1 or the number itself; if the number produced is prime, the next person adds 7.

For example: 56, 7, 14, 2, 9, 3, 10, 5, 12, . . .

Can the children . . .

point out simple patterns? (for example, when counting in twos from 0, tell you that the pattern is 2, 4, 6, 8, 0, . . .)

level 2

point out the patterns when counting in fives and tens from 0?

point out the patterns when counting in twos, fives and tens from 1 or another number?

level 3

point out the patterns when counting in any single-digit number from 0?

point out the patterns when counting in any single-digit number from 1 or another number?

continue the patterns when counting above 100?

record the number series in such a way that the patterns show up?

level 4

predict the patterns when counting in any single-digit number from 0?

predict the patterns when counting in any single-digit number from 1 or another number?

level 5

JUMP FROM WHERE?

Children will experience

◆ looking for number patterns
◆ predicting numbers using their knowledge of number patterns
◆ practice in using a number line

Equipment

◆ 0-100 number line
◆ decimal number line
◆ blank number line
◆ felt-tipped pens
◆ two dice
◆ pencil and paper

Getting started

You can introduce this activity to a group, then split the children up into pairs.

● One child tosses a dice to find where to start on the line, and rings that number (with younger children you may want them to omit this, and start all their jump series from 0)
● The other child tosses both dice and adds the numbers together (or subtracts) to find the size of jump to draw
● The children then work together to draw jumps of this size from their starting-point, until they can go no further
● They should record on a piece of paper the numbers where they land

Older or more able children could explore jumping on a decimal number line, or a line showing both positive and negative numbers.

Questions to ask the children

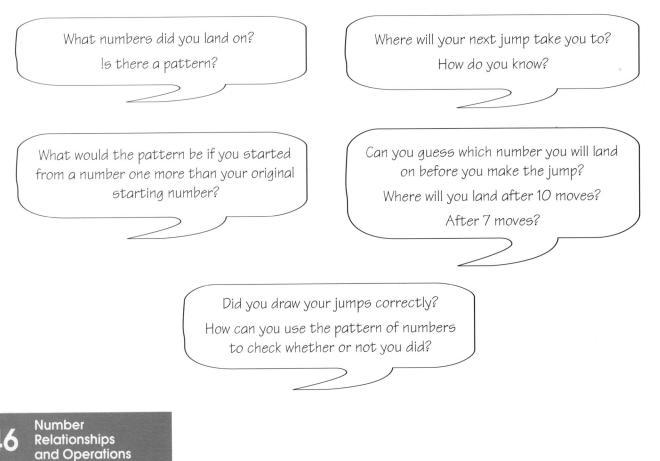

What numbers did you land on?
Is there a pattern?

Where will your next jump take you to?
How do you know?

What would the pattern be if you started from a number one more than your original starting number?

Can you guess which number you will land on before you make the jump?
Where will you land after 10 moves?
After 7 moves?

Did you draw your jumps correctly?
How can you use the pattern of numbers to check whether or not you did?

Keeping going

◆ Children can jump backwards from 100 or numbers near 100.

◆ Children can work on a line numbered from –50 to +50.

◆ Children can predict where they would land if their line continued past 100. Ask them how they can check whether their predictions are correct.

◆ Children can toss two dice and find their product (for example, 4 and 6 — product 24). They mark this number on the line and find all the ways of reaching there in equal jumps from 0.

Can the children . . .

draw jumps of any size from 1 to 6 accurately on the number line?

point out the pattern made by jumps of 2, from 0 or another number — up to 20?

level 2

point out and discuss the pattern made by jumps of 5, from 0 or another number — up to 100?

point out and discuss the pattern made by jumps of 10, from 0 or another number — up to 100?

predict the pattern made by jumps of 2, from 0 up to 20?

predict the pattern made by jumps of 5, from 0 up to 50?

predict the pattern made by jumps of 10, from 0 up to 100?

level 3

predict the pattern made by jumps of 5, from 0 or another number — up to 100?

predict the pattern made by jumps of 10, from 0 or another number — up to 100?

point out and discuss the pattern made by jumps of any single-digit number, from 0 or another number — up to 100?

level 4

point out and discuss the pattern made by jumping on a decimal number line?

point out and discuss the pattern made by jumping on a negative number line?

level 5

KEEP ON GOING

Children will experience
- familiarity with number patterns
- predicting numbers using their knowledge of number patterns
- making generalisations

Equipment
- overhead projector calculator
- a large display calculator
- ordinary calculators
- blackboard
- number line
- paper and pencil

Getting started

This activity can be done with the whole class or with a group.

You need a calculator whose display everyone can see, such as an overhead projector calculator, or a large display one — or you could use a calculator of normal size and write up the 'answers' on a blackboard.

Get one of the children to suggest a fairly simple 'sum' such as $12 \div 2$. Do the operation on the calculator and show the children the answer, then keep doing the same operation (in this case, $\div 2 =$), and show the pattern of numbers produced (6, 3, 1.5, 0.75, . . .).

Discuss with the children what is happening to the numbers in the display.

Questions to ask the children

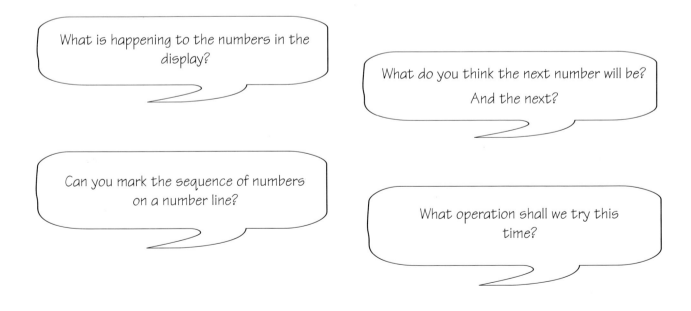

What is happening to the numbers in the display?

What do you think the next number will be? And the next?

Can you mark the sequence of numbers on a number line?

What operation shall we try this time?

Keeping going

◆ Children can work in pairs on this activity, taking it in turns to choose a 'sum' to explore.

◆ Encourage children to explore at least one of each operation, + – x and ÷.

◆ Children can use a spreadsheet to continue the number patterns they have made, or to explore new ones.

Can the children . . .

make a general statement such as 'The numbers are getting smaller' or 'Each one is being multiplied by 3'?
level 2

make sensible predictions about the next number in the series when using addition or subtraction?
make sensible predictions about the next number in the series when multiplying or dividing by 2 or 10?
level 3

estimate the next number in the series when multiplying or dividing by 2 or 10?
predict the next number in the series when multiplying or dividing by numbers other than 2 or 10?
make sensible predictions about the next number in the series when multiplying by 100 or 1000?
level 4

estimate the next number in the series when working with decimal or negative numbers?
make sensible predictions about the next number in the series when dividing by 100 or 1000?
level 5

MONTY

Children will experience
- familiarity with number patterns
- predicting numbers using their knowledge of number patterns

Equipment
- software: 'Monty' in *Slimwam 2*

Getting started

'Monty' is a game for a pair or a small group where the aim is to identify the number pattern of a grid.

Children are presented with number grids of varying patterns. When they have looked at the grid, this disappears and a python called Monty moves across the screen. The child stops Monty by pressing the space bar, at which point one of the numbers 'under' Monty's body reappears; the task is to work out the other numbers 'under' the python's body.

Questions to ask the children

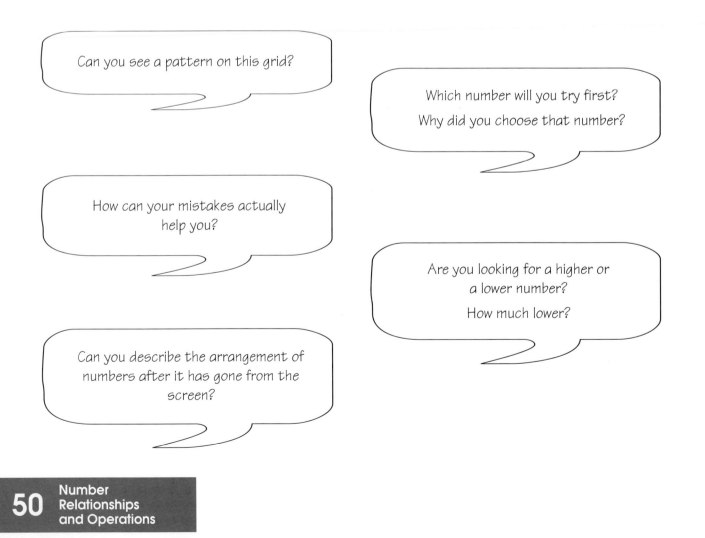

Can you see a pattern on this grid?

Which number will you try first?
Why did you choose that number?

How can your mistakes actually help you?

Are you looking for a higher or a lower number?
How much lower?

Can you describe the arrangement of numbers after it has gone from the screen?

Keeping going

◆ One child sets the grid and their partner finds the numbers.

◆ Children can try to find Monty's numbers without looking at the number grid first.

◆ Children can make their own grids on squared paper (at a wide range of levels of difficulty). They cover numbers up with linking cubes or a paper shape (for example an ∟ or ⊤) for their friends to guess.

Can the children . . .

read numbers up to 100?

write numbers 1 to 100 in order?

recognise sequences of numbers?

create their own grids using numbers 1 to 100?

level 2

spot patterns and predict the next in the series?

mentally recall the multiplication bonds in the 2, 5 and 10 multiplication tables?

mentally recall the multiplication bonds up to 5 x 5?

use mental recall of addition and subtraction facts to solve problems with larger numbers?

level 3

create their own grids using addition and multiplication to make number patterns?

mentally recall multiplication bonds up to 10 x 10?

level 4

create their own grids using any of the four operations to make number patterns?

create their own grids using fractional and decimal numbers?

level 5

MATCHSTICKS

Children will experience

◆ looking for rules and patterns
◆ predicting numbers using their knowledge of number patterns
◆ making generalisations
◆ counting in number series

Equipment

◆ headless matches
◆ short sticks of uniform length
◆ paper and pencil

Getting started

You can introduce this activity to a group or the whole class.

Children use matches to make a series of squares. They should record how many matches are needed for 1 square, for 2 squares, and so on. They can also explore 'growing' squares in a variety of ways.

1 square needs 4
2 squares need 8
3 squares need 12
4 squares need 16

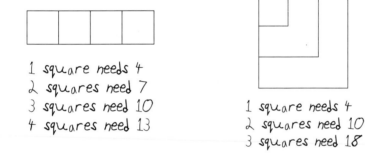

1 square needs 4
2 squares need 7
3 squares need 10
4 squares need 13

1 square needs 4
2 squares need 10
3 squares need 18

Questions to ask the children

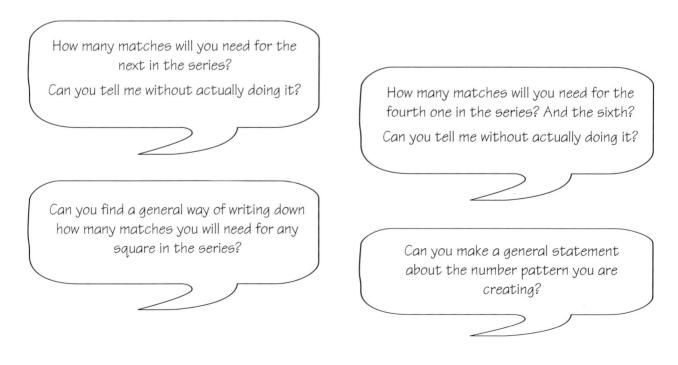

How many matches will you need for the next in the series?

Can you tell me without actually doing it?

How many matches will you need for the fourth one in the series? And the sixth?

Can you tell me without actually doing it?

Can you find a general way of writing down how many matches you will need for any square in the series?

Can you make a general statement about the number pattern you are creating?

Keeping going

◆ Children can make a series of triangles or other shapes, and explore them in the same way as the squares.

◆ Children can make a series of squares that get ever larger.

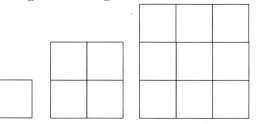

Can the children . . .

count on from where they are, rather than returning to the beginning each time?

count large numbers accurately?

keep track when counting large numbers?

say how many more matchsticks are needed each time with a simple pattern such as this?

level 2

check their work when counting large numbers?

make general statements such as 'It's the numbers in the 4 times table'

or 'You need four and then three more for each square'?

level 3

predict how many will be needed for the 10th in the series?

level 4

predict how many will be needed for the 100th in the series?

make general statements about the patterns which will enable them to find the number of matchsticks needed anywhere in the series?

level 5

COLOURED SQUARES

Children will experience

◆ familiarity with recognising and producing patterns
◆ making generalisations
◆ making predictions

Equipment

◆ squared paper ($^1/_2$ cm, 1 cm or 2 cm)
◆ scissors
◆ coloured pens or pencils

Getting started

This activity can be done with groups or the whole class.

Ask children to make a repeating pattern such as 'red blue green, red blue green' by colouring in a strip of squared paper.

| red | blue | green | red | blue | green | red | blue |

Can they predict what colour the tenth square will be? And the 25th square? The 100th?

They can explore other repeating patterns such as r b b g, r b b g or y r g r y, y r g r y.

Questions to ask the children

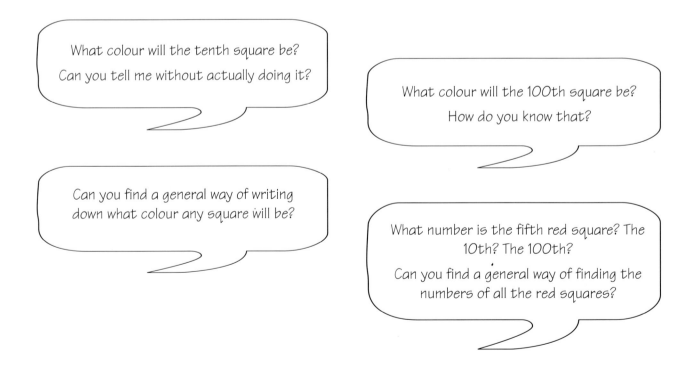

What colour will the tenth square be?
Can you tell me without actually doing it?

What colour will the 100th square be?
How do you know that?

Can you find a general way of writing down what colour any square will be?

What number is the fifth red square? The 10th? The 100th?
Can you find a general way of finding the numbers of all the red squares?

Keeping going

◆ Children can make combination patterns — for example, rbg, rbg, rr, rbg, rbg, rr, . . .

◆ Children can make patterns on strips of paper two squares wide.

◆ Children can make patterns using isometric (triangle) paper.

◆ One child makes up a pattern in secret, then gives some clues about it to the others. Such clues might be: 'There are just three colours; the second square is red; the fifth is red and the tenth is blue'. The others try to work out what the pattern could be and whether there is more than one possibility.

Can the children . . .

say what colour the tenth square will be without actually colouring that far?

level 2

say what colour the 100th square will be without actually colouring that far?

say how they worked it out?

level 3

say what colour any square will be without actually colouring that far?

say where, for example, the third or the tenth red square will be without actually colouring that far?

say how they worked it out?

level 4

find a general way of writing down what colour any square will be?

level 5

Operations: Addition and Subtraction

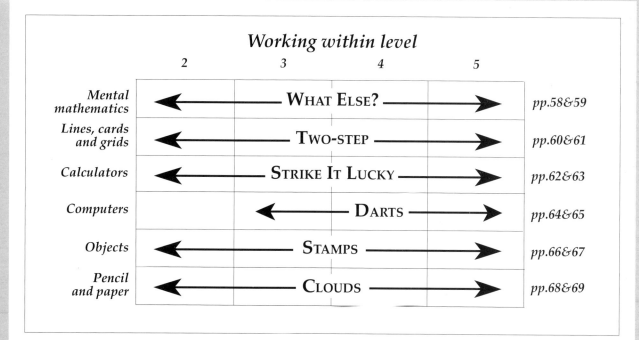

	Working within level			
	2	3	4	5	
Mental mathematics	◄─────── WHAT ELSE? ───────►				*pp.58&59*
Lines, cards and grids	◄─────── TWO-STEP ───────►				*pp.60&61*
Calculators	◄─────── STRIKE IT LUCKY ───────►				*pp.62&63*
Computers	◄─── DARTS ───────►				*pp.64&65*
Objects	◄─────── STAMPS ───────►				*pp.66&67*
Pencil and paper	◄─────── CLOUDS ───────►				*pp.68&69*

What Else?

Children will experience

◆ estimating

◆ calculating mentally

◆ thinking logically and systematically

◆ equivalence

Equipment

◆ calculators

◆ pencil and paper

Getting started

This activity can be done in groups or with the whole class. Choose a number operation that is 'easy' for the children, and ask them to help you use it to deduce further addition and subtraction facts.

For example if 36 + 14 = 50, then the following must be true:

$$30 + 6 + 14 = 50$$
$$37 + 14 = 51$$
$$51 - 14 = 37$$

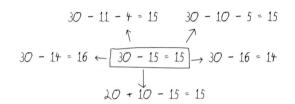

When children are sure of what they are doing, ask them to think of a number operation that is a bit hard for them, or to look in their books to find a recent calculation that was.

They then use that to deduce further number facts.

Questions to ask the children

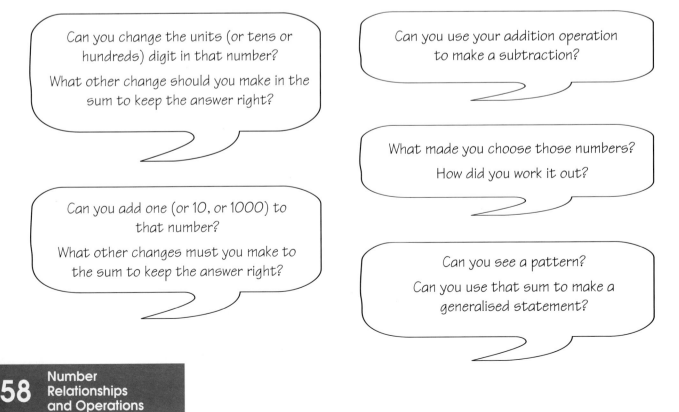

Can you change the units (or tens or hundreds) digit in that number?
What other change should you make in the sum to keep the answer right?

Can you add one (or 10, or 1000) to that number?
What other changes must you make to the sum to keep the answer right?

Can you use your addition operation to make a subtraction?

What made you choose those numbers?
How did you work it out?

Can you see a pattern?
Can you use that sum to make a generalised statement?

Keeping going

◆ When children are confident about what they are doing, many will be able to work with higher numbers.

◆ Explore with the children all the ways they can think of to work out a problem mentally — for example, 26 + 19.

◆ Children can work with multiplication and division or with mixed operations.

$$2 + (10 \times 5) = 52$$

so

$$10 \times 5 = 52 - 2$$

Can the children . . .

make an addition sum into a subtraction or vice versa? (for example, starting with 23 + 15 = 38, deduce that 38 – 15 = 23)

level 2

understand that when adding any number to (or subtracting it from) one side of the equation you must do the same to the other side? (for example, if 25 + 25 + 25 = 75, then 25 + 25 = 75 – 25)

explain their work?

level 3

use strategies learnt in this activity to help solve mental problems? (for example, when working out 74 – 27, know that adding three to each side will give 77 – 30, which is easier to do)

level 4

starting from any sum, make a generalised statement about what can be deduced from it? (for example, '25 add 125 makes 150, so I can increase the numbers on both sides by any number and the sum is still true: 25 + 125 + n = 150 + n')

level 5

TWO-STEP

Children will experience

♦ halving numbers
♦ mental calculation
♦ odd and even numbers

Equipment

♦ 0-100 number lines
♦ –50 to +50 number lines
♦ unnumbered number lines
♦ decimal or fraction number lines

Getting started

Children work in pairs. Each child chooses a number and marks it on the number line. They then work together to explore ways of getting from one number to the other in two jumps (either of different sizes, or the same size).

The lines you provide will indicate to children the range of numbers they should work with (negative, 0-100, fraction or decimal). More able children can use unnumbered lines and decide what numbers to put at the markers on their line.

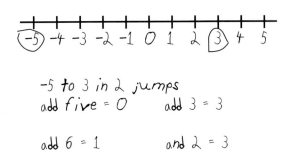

Questions to ask the children

How else could you get from that number to the other using two jumps?

How can you record your jumps?

Could you get from one number to the other using two jumps of the same size?

How do you know that?

If you jumped backwards, from the higher to the lower number, what size jumps might you do then?

How many different-sized jumps can you make from one number to the other?

Are there any other ways you could do it?

How do you know?

Keeping going

◆ Children can work with different number lines.

◆ Ask children: How many ways are there of making two different-sized jumps from 0 to 20? 0 to 50 or 100?

◆ Once children are familiar with the activity, number lines are not necessary. They can work mentally or with pencil and paper to calculate their jumps, then check using a calculator.

◆ Children can investigate systematically the equal pairs of jumps that can be made from 0. That is, two jumps of one land on 2; two jumps of two land on 4, and so on.

◆ Another way to look at the above problem is to take each whole number in turn and work out how to reach it in two equal jumps — which involves working with halves.

To reach 1   0.5 + 0.5
To reach 2   1 + 1
To reach 3   1.5 + 1.5

Can the children . . .

get from one number to another on a 0-100 number line using two jumps?

get from one number to another on a 0-100 number line using two jumps of the same size?

record their work?

say that jumping backwards from the higher to the lower number can be done with the same size jumps as when moving from the lower to the higher?

level 2

work out how to get from any number to another using two jumps in the region 0-100 — mentally or on paper?

get from any number to another using two jumps on a negative number line and record their work?

find more than one way of getting from one number to another using two jumps?

level 3

work out how to get from any whole number to another using two jumps in the region 0-1000 — mentally or on paper?

get from one number to another on a decimal number line using two jumps of any size?

find all the ways of getting from one number to another using two (whole number) jumps?

explain how they know they have found all the ways?

record their work?

level 4

get from one number to another on a fraction number line using two jumps of any size?

get from any whole number to another in two equal jumps, using fractions or decimals as necessary? (for example, 5 to 10 can be done with two jumps of 2.5)

record their work using conventional equations? (for example, 5 + 2.5 + 2.5 = 10)

level 5

STRIKE IT LUCKY

Children will experience
◆ predicting
◆ mental calculation

Equipment
◆ calculators
◆ cards 0-50 or 0-50 chart
◆ pencil and paper

Getting started
Children work in twos or threes.

● In secret, each child chooses three 'lucky numbers' under 100 and writes these down
● They share a calculator and set it to 50
● Now the children take it in turn to pick a number between 0 and 50 (each number can be chosen *only once*, so they will need to use number cards and turn them over when they are used, or cross out numbers on a chart.) The player adds this number to, or subtracts it from, the running total on the calculator. (It may help to keep a record of the total on paper too, in case of accidents with the calculator.)
● Whenever the calculator displays a player's 'lucky number' they can tick it on their papers
● When someone has all three numbers ticked, they win

Questions to ask the children

What would be a good number to choose to add or subtract?

Can you think of a way to help you reach one of your lucky numbers?

Why did you chose those lucky numbers?

Were they a good choice?

What might you choose next time?

Why did you choose that number to add (or subtract)?

Did it achieve what you hoped?

Can you guess what number your partner is trying to get?

Keeping going

◆ A variation of this game is to have the lucky numbers out in the open, not secret.

◆ The game can be a collaborative exercise, with the aim being to cross off everybody's three lucky numbers.

◆ In a more challenging version of this game the numbers children can add or subtract is limited — perhaps odd numbers only, or numbers 0-20.

◆ Put a time limit on choosing a number to add or subtract — say, 5 seconds.

◆ Children can choose numbers for their friends. (This avoids them choosing 'easy' ones, which can happen as they become familiar with the game.)

◆ Set the calculator to 100, 150 or 500 to start with.

◆ Children can work with higher numbers, decimal numbers, or negative numbers.

Can the children . . .

play the game, choosing numbers to add or subtract fairly randomly, and recognising when they have hit one of their 'lucky numbers'?

level 2

play the game, choosing what number to add or subtract with some care?

make sensible estimates about what adding or subtracting a particular number will do to the number in the calculator display?

say why they have chosen a particular number to add or subtract?

level 3

say what adding or subtracting a particular number will do to the number in the calculator display?

invent variations to the game and explain them?

level 4

develop and use strategies for playing the game?

level 5

DARTS

Children will experience

- developing strategies for mental calculation
- computation involving all four operations
- developing systems for checking their calculations

Equipment

- software: 'Darts' in *The Next 17* from SMILE
- calculators
- pencil and paper

Getting started

'Darts' is a game for two whose purpose is to encourage children to calculate mentally.

A dart board is drawn on the screen and each player starts with 501 points. The aim, as in conventional darts, is to get your score to zero. Each player 'throws' three darts. After three shots players subtract their score from their total. The first person to get to zero is the winner. Players can challenge each other if they disagree with a calculation and if the challenge is correct the player making the error does not score that round. An incorrect challenge gives 50 penalty points. The game can be played against the computer.

Questions to ask the children

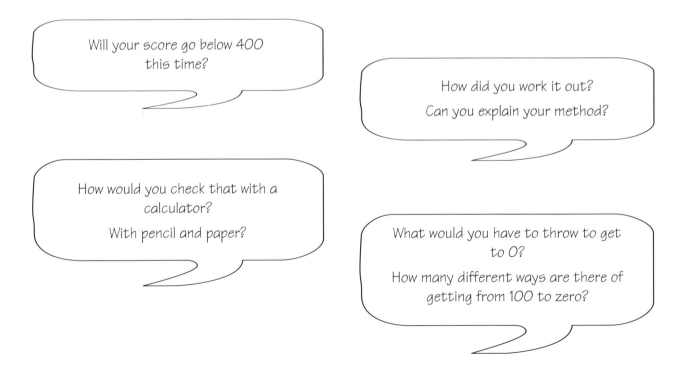

Will your score go below 400 this time?

How did you work it out?
Can you explain your method?

How would you check that with a calculator?
With pencil and paper?

What would you have to throw to get to 0?
How many different ways are there of getting from 100 to zero?

Keeping going

◆ Children can play 'Boxes 4' (see the other Boxes games on page 8).

◆ Children can play 'Minimax' from SMILE's *The Next 17*. This is an activity played against the computer to reinforce their understanding of place value, and practise skills of estimation and of operating with addition, subtraction and multiplication.

Children choose whether to add, subtract or multiply, and whether they are aiming at a maximum or minimum number. A board appears with an operation drawn on it, but with the numbers missing. Five integers between 1 and 9 are displayed one at a time and children decide where to place each one on the board. When all five integers are in place the computer performs the calculation and shows children whether they managed to make the number required.

Can the children . . .

not appropriate
level 2

do the calculations using their own pencil and paper methods?
make a sensible estimate of where their next score will take them, to the nearest 100?
level 3

do the calculations mentally?
make a sensible estimate of where their next score will take them, to the nearest 10?
level 4

model their calculations involving doubles and trebles using a calculator?
write down their calculations using brackets?
level 5

STAMPS

Children will experience

- developing strategies for mental calculation
- computation involving multiplication and addition
- developing systems for checking their calculations

Equipment

- used stamps
- sheet of unused stamps, borrowed from the school office, to show the children
- photocopied sheets of stamps for the children to cut up (for example, 2p and 5p stamps)

Getting started

This activity can be done with a group or the whole class.

Give the children sheets of stamps in two different amounts. Ask them to find out what different amounts they can make by combining two or more stamps.

Older children can go on to work without actual stamps.

(levels 2 & 3)   2p and 5p stamps or 6p and 4p stamps

(levels 4 & 5)   20p and 26p stamps

Questions to ask the children

How many total amounts up to £1 can you make?

Can you make 10p? 11p? 12p? . . .

Are there any amounts you can't make?

What amounts could you make with just 2p stamps?

With just 5p stamps?

How many amounts can you make up to £5 with 20p and 26p stamps?

Are there any amounts you can't make?

Can you write a rule stating which sums you can make with 20p and 26p stamps?

Keeping going

◆ A similar exploration can be done with coins — what sums can you pay for with just 5p and 2p coins (or 10p and 5p, or 20p and 50p . . .).

◆ Children can find out at a post office what denomination of stamps are available and make up their own problems based on these.

◆ Children can explore what sums can be made with *three* denominations of coin or stamp.

Can the children . . .

work at random, adding amounts together?

find one or more ways to make a specific sum, such as 10p or 20p?

level 2

find several ways to make a specific sum, such as 20p or 50p?

find how many total amounts up to £1 can be made?

find any total amounts up to £1 that cannot be made?

level 3

find all the sums under £5 that can be made with two stamps of a particular value, such as 12p and 15p?

be systematic in tackling a problem?

explain how they know they have 'found all the possibilities'?

level 4

write a rule stating which sums can be made with two stamps of a particular value, such as 12p and 15p?

level 5

CLOUDS

Children will experience

- estimation
- algorithms for solving vertical number problems
- using and strengthening an understanding of place value
- trial and improvement methods

Equipment

- paper and pencil
- calculators

Getting started

Give children number problems where one or more of the numbers is obscured by a 'cloud'. Ask them to discover the hidden numbers.

Initially, give problems with just one cloud, where only one answer is possible. Later, move on to problems with two or more clouds — what are all the possible answers? You can also obscure the operation sign.

$$
\begin{array}{r}
1\Box \\
+\ 25 \\
\hline
39
\end{array}
\qquad
\begin{array}{r}
3\Box \\
-\Box7 \\
\hline
12
\end{array}
\qquad
\begin{array}{r}
15 \\
\times\ 1\Box \\
\hline
\Box8\Box
\end{array}
\qquad
\begin{array}{r}
90 \\
\Box4 \\
\hline
22.5
\end{array}
$$

Questions to ask the children

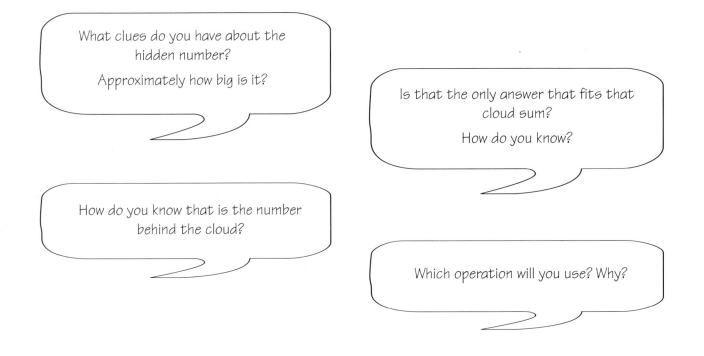

What clues do you have about the hidden number?

Approximately how big is it?

Is that the only answer that fits that cloud sum?

How do you know?

How do you know that is the number behind the cloud?

Which operation will you use? Why?

Keeping going

◆ Children can make up cloud sums for their friends — but make it a rule that they must be able to solve them themselves!

◆ Children can make up number problems where the answer is 10. What are all the possibilities?

Can the children . . .

solve addition and subtraction problems up to 10 without the aid of a calculator — where the operation is known and there is only one solution?

solve addition and subtraction problems up to 50 with the aid of a calculator — where the operation is known and there is only one solution?

level 2

solve addition and subtraction problems involving two- and three-digit numbers with the aid of a calculator — where the operation is known and there is only one solution?

solve multiplication and division problems involving one- and two-digit numbers with the aid of a calculator — where the operation is known and there is only one solution?

level 3

solve addition and subtraction problems involving two- or three-digit numbers *without* the aid of a calculator — whether or not the operation is known and whether there are one or more solutions?

solve multiplication and division problems with the aid of a calculator — whether or not the operation is known and whether there are one or more solutions?

use clues to work out the operation when it is hidden?

level 4

solve problems involving two- to four-digit numbers without the aid of a calculator — whether or not the operation is known and whether there are one or more solutions?

work out when there is insufficient information to solve a problem?

level 5

Operations: Multiplication and Division

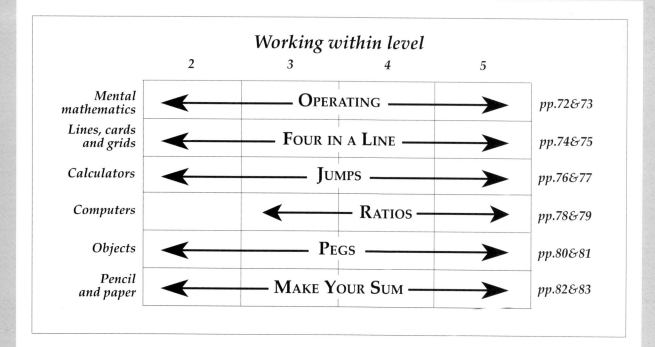

	Working within level			
	2	**3**	**4**	**5**
Mental mathematics	◄———————— OPERATING ————————►				pp.72&73
Lines, cards and grids	◄———————— FOUR IN A LINE ————————►				pp.74&75
Calculators	◄———————— JUMPS ————————►				pp.76&77
Computers	◄———— RATIOS ————►				pp.78&79
Objects	◄———————— PEGS ————————►				pp.80&81
Pencil and paper	◄———————— MAKE YOUR SUM ————————►				pp.82&83

OPERATING

Children will experience
- practising mental multiplication and division
- predicting
- estimating

Equipment
- number cards 0-9
- number cards 0-100
- paper and pencil
- multiplication charts
- role cards — 'chooser', 'operator' and 'guesser' (optional)

Getting started

This an activity for a group of three children, each child with a role: 'chooser', 'operator' or 'guesser'. You can introduce it to a group or the whole class before splitting the children up into threes.

- The group first needs to agree on a simple multiplication or division operation such as 'x 3'
- The chooser then picks a mystery number under 10, writes it down in secret, and hands it to the operator, who does the operation (in this case, multiplies the number by three) mentally
- The operator tells the guesser the result
- The guesser, who knows only the operation and the result, must guess what the mystery number was

Children should take turns at different roles and, when they are confident with the activity, move on to working with division, with more than one operation, or with higher starter numbers.

Questions to ask the children

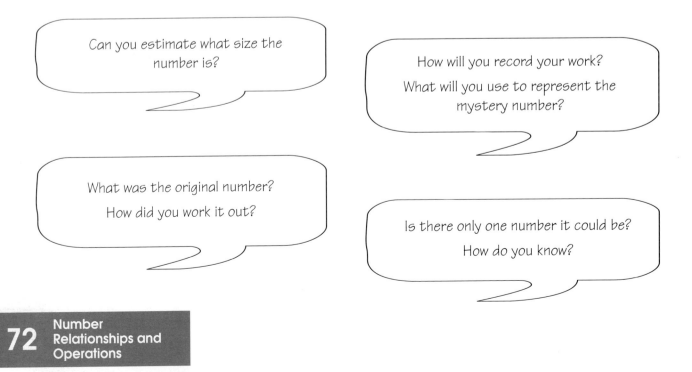

Can you estimate what size the number is?

How will you record your work?
What will you use to represent the mystery number?

What was the original number?
How did you work it out?

Is there only one number it could be?
How do you know?

Keeping going

- Let children use a calculator and work with starter numbers over 20. (Older and more able children can use these higher numbers and still work mentally.)

- Children can make their own multiplication charts to help them in this game.

- Children can work in groups of four, with two operators, working in turn on the number that is passed to them, like a production line.

  If $x + 3 \times 5 = 35$, what is x?

  (The guesser may well need a calculator for this version.)

- More able children can use negative and decimal numbers.

Can the children . . .

find the original number when the operation was addition or subtraction of a single-digit number?

make a sensible estimate of the original number when the operation was addition or subtraction of a two-digit number?

make a sensible estimate of the original number when the operation was 'x 2' or '÷ 2'?

level 2

find the original number when the operation was multiplication or division in the 2, 5 or 10 multiplication tables?

find the original number when the operation was multiplication (or division) up to 5 x 5 (or 25 ÷ 5)?

make a sensible estimate of the original number when they cannot give the exact answer?

explain in simple terms how they worked out the number? (for example, 'I know that 2 x 3 is 6, so I knew it was 3')

level 3

find the original number when the operation was multiplication or division in any of the multiplication tables up to 10 x 10?

level 4

make a sensible estimate of the original number when working with negative and decimal numbers?

level 5

Four in a Line

Children will experience
◆ practising mental multiplication and division
◆ developing strategies

Equipment
◆ squared paper (2 cm or 5 cm)
◆ number cards 1-20
◆ calculator (optional)
◆ counters

Getting started

Children should work in pairs. Each pair needs an 8 x 8 grid and a pack of well-shuffled number cards.

● The children take turns to pick two cards, multiply the numbers together, and write the answer in any square of the grid, continuing until each square is filled

● They then shuffle the entire pack of cards again and, in turn, pick the top two cards; multiply those numbers together; place a counter on that number on the grid (if it appears there); then put the cards to the bottom of the pack

● The first person to complete a line of four (horizontally, vertically or diagonally) is the winner

(For a simpler game, where children are still working within level 2, replace multiplication by addition and/or finding the difference.)

Questions to ask the children

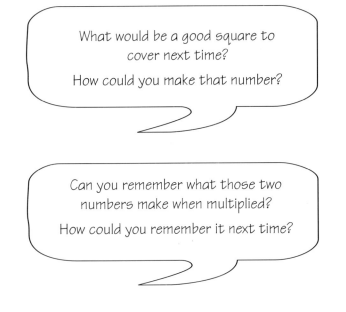

What would be a good square to cover next time?

How could you make that number?

What do you get when you multiply those two numbers together?

How can you work it out?

Can you remember what those two numbers make when multiplied?

How could you remember it next time?

Keeping going

◆ The game can be played just as well using division as well as (or instead of) multiplication — both when writing the numbers in the grid, and when making lines of four.

◆ Children can work collaboratively, aiming to complete as many rows of four as they can.

◆ Children can each use counters in a different colour, and aim to make a line of four in their colour.

◆ Children can clear the grid of counters after each line is completed, or they can go on to make three lines of four, or as many as they can.

Can the children . . .

play the game using addition or subtraction instead of multiplication?

say what would be a good square to cover next time?

level 2

play the game using multiplication, with some help from a calculator?

say how to make any number in the 2, 5 or 10 multiplication tables?

say how to make any number in the multiplication tables up to 5 x 5?

level 3

play the game using multiplication or division, with some help from a calculator?

recall how to make any number in the multiplication tables up to 10 x 10?

find a way of working out any number up to 20 x 20, mentally or on paper?

level 4

identify all their possible options for getting four in a line?

say which card-numbers they need in order to make any of these numbers?

level 5

JUMPS

Children will experience

- exploring all the ways of factorising a number
- looking at prime numbers
- working with multiplication and division
- working systematically

Equipment

- calculators
- number lines to 30 and 100 (levels 2 to 4)
- decimal number lines (level 5)

Getting started

This activity can be introduced to the whole class or a group.

Children work in groups of two or three. Everybody in the group thinks of a different single- or two-digit number. (Older children could use only two-digit numbers.) These two or three numbers are then multiplied together to make the target number.

The group then works together to find all the ways of reaching that number from 0 in equal-sized jumps. For example, to reach a target of 50, children can jump in 2s, 5s, 10s or 25s.

I jumped to 48 on the calculator. First I jumped in 8s

8
16
24
32
40
48

Questions to ask the children

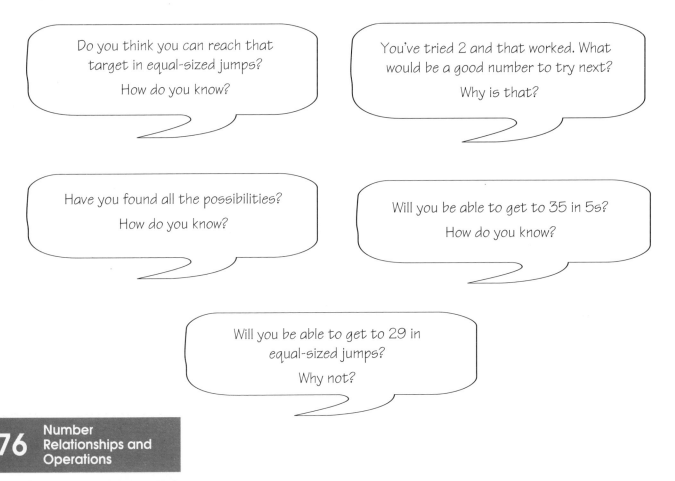

Do you think you can reach that target in equal-sized jumps?

How do you know?

You've tried 2 and that worked. What would be a good number to try next?

Why is that?

Have you found all the possibilities?

How do you know?

Will you be able to get to 35 in 5s?

How do you know?

Will you be able to get to 29 in equal-sized jumps?

Why not?

Keeping going

◆ Children can work in pairs. Each child chooses a three-digit number for the other to analyse — how many ways can you reach it in equal jumps?

◆ Children can explore which numbers can never be reached in equal-sized jumps. What are these numbers called?

Can the children . . .

use the calculator to jump from 0 to 20 in 2s and 5s?

describe the pattern the numbers make?

level 2

predict whether it is possible to jump from 0 to 20 in 2s, from 0 to 50 in 5s, and from 0 to 100 in 10s?

predict whether it is possible to jump from 0 to 16 in 4s?

say some other-sized jumps that would also work?

level 3

make sensible estimates of what is possible when jumping from 0 to any number under 100 using any single-digit number?

discuss which numbers cannot be reached with equal-sized jumps, and name these 'prime numbers'?

level 4

make equal-sized jumps on a decimal line with intervals of 0.1?

make sensible predictions about which numbers can be reached with equal-sized jumps on a line with intervals of 0.1? (for example, say that starting at 0 and making jumps of 0.5 they will reach 9 but not 9.3)

level 5

RATIOS

Children will experience

- using simple formulae to solve problems
- developing accuracy in measurement
- developing an understanding of decimals in the context of measurement
- experiencing ratios in a practical situation

Equipment

- any spreadsheet program

Getting started

In this activity children find out some personal measurements and then investigate the ratios between them, asking questions such as 'How many hand spans tall are you?'.

Ask the children to measure their heights and handspans. Discuss with them the best way of calculating the ratio of handspan to height and what formula they might need to use.

The results of the group (or the whole class) should be entered into a spreadsheet; comparisons can then be made and the range of the data used to make some generalised statements.

Once the data has been entered and the ratios calculated pupils should examine the data to make comparisons.

Encourage them to ask questions and try to find answers.

name	handspan (cm)	height (cm)	spans tall
Anthea	17	138	8.12
Ishmael	16	129	8.06
Judy	15.5		
Teo			
Julia			

Questions to ask the children

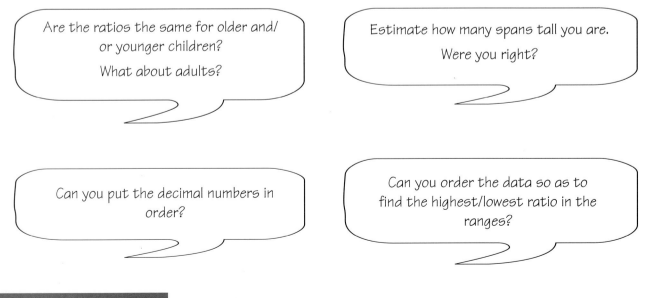

Are the ratios the same for older and/ or younger children?
What about adults?

Estimate how many spans tall you are. Were you right?

Can you put the decimal numbers in order?

Can you order the data so as to find the highest/lowest ratio in the ranges?

Keeping going

◆ Ask the children, "Does the tallest person have the longest foot?" or "Do people with long feet have long hands?"

◆ Children can use Imperial measures to repeat an investigation. Are the ratios still the same? Should they be?

◆ Other questions to investigate are "How many of your feet tall are you?", "How many cubits tall are you?".

Can the children . . .

not appropriate
level 2

measure body parts to the nearest centimetre?
understand the relationship between muliplication and division?
level 3

measure body parts to the nearest millimetre?
use decimal notation to record measurements?
level 4

use mental methods for multiplying and dividing whole numbers?
use simple formulae to solve problems?
level 5

PEGS

Children will experience

◆ relationship between multiplication and division
◆ exploring all the ways of factorising a number
◆ looking at prime numbers

Equipment

◆ pegs
◆ pegboards
◆ pencil and paper

Getting started

Each child needs a pegboard and 36 pegs. Ask them to find out all the different ways the pegs can be arranged to form rows of equal length.

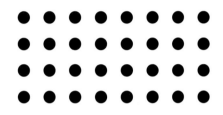

Once children have completed this, they can choose any number under 100 to explore in the same way.

(To simplify the activity for children who are not very confident, choose numbers such as 12, 10 or 15 before asking them to move on to 36.)

Questions to ask the children

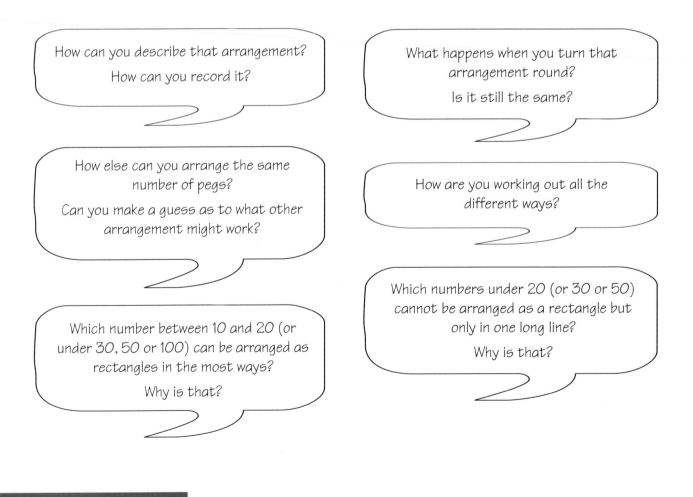

How can you describe that arrangement?
How can you record it?

What happens when you turn that arrangement round?
Is it still the same?

How else can you arrange the same number of pegs?
Can you make a guess as to what other arrangement might work?

How are you working out all the different ways?

Which number between 10 and 20 (or under 30, 50 or 100) can be arranged as rectangles in the most ways?
Why is that?

Which numbers under 20 (or 30 or 50) cannot be arranged as a rectangle but only in one long line?
Why is that?

Keeping going

◆ Children could explore the same problems by arranging square tiles, or shading squares on paper.

◆ A group of children could mark on a 1-100 chart how many ways each number can be arranged as a rectangle. Which numbers can only be arranged in a line? What kind of numbers are these?

Can the children . . .

arrange their pegs in a rectangular array and write a sentence to describe it?   *level 2*

rearrange their pegs to make a second rectangular array (where this is possible) and write a number sentence to describe it? recognise that an arrangement such as 5 rows of 6 can also give 6 rows of 5?   *level 3*

be systematic in finding all the ways of arranging a number of pegs such as 24 or 36? explain how they know they have found all the possibilities? discuss those numbers which will not make a rectangular array, but only a line, and name them as 'prime numbers'? recognise that a rectangular array can be described by a division as well as a multiplication sentence (for example, a 5 x 6 array is also 30 ÷ 5 or 30 ÷ 6) *level 4*

explore the question 'Which number of pegs under 50 can be arranged in the most ways?' and find an answer?   *level 5*

MAKE YOUR SUM

Children will experience

◆ working with multiplication and division

◆ working systematically

Equipment

◆ pencil and paper

◆ sets of number cards, or photocopied sheets of numbers

◆ multiplication and division cards

[×] [÷]

◆ calculator (at the discretion of the teacher)

Getting started

Give children some multiplication and division cards and a set of related numbers. Ask them to make and complete as many number sentences as they can using just those numbers and the multiplication and division symbols.

Possible sets are as follows:

(level 2)   2 10 20 5   or   2   3   6   12

(level 3)   12 6 2 3 4 24

(level 4)   all the numbers from one of the multiplication tables, or

a set of single-digit numbers and 10 and 100 (making their own 'answer' cards), or

single-digit and two-digit numbers (again making their own 'answer' cards)

(level 5)   a set of single- or two-digit numbers and 10, 100 and 1000 (no 'answer' cards), or

single-digit, two-digit and three-digit numbers (no 'answer' cards), or

2 4 5 0.8 0.5

My numbers are 12 6 2 3 4 24

$2 \times 6 = 12$ $2 \times 3 = 6$

$12 \div 3 = 4$ $6 \times 2 = 12$

$6 \div 2 = 3$ $4 \times 3 = 12$

Questions to ask the children

Why have you not divided that number? Could you divide it by one of the others?

Can you estimate what the answer will be?

Can you see any pattern?

Keeping going

◆ You can include some fractions in the cards you give the children.

◆ Children can use the x and ÷ cards together in the same sum.

◆ Children can think of a way to make the activity into a game.

Can the children . . .

make up addition and subtraction sums using the numbers 2, 5, 10 and 20?

level 2

make up multiplication sums using the numbers 2, 5, 10 and 20?

make up multiplication sums using the numbers 12, 6, 2, 3, 4 and 24?

level 3

make up multiplication and division sums using all the numbers from one of the multiplication tables?

make up multiplication and division sums using a set of single-digit numbers and 10 and 100?

make up multiplication and division sums using single-digit and two-digit numbers?

level 4

make up multiplication and division sums using a set of single- or two-digit numbers and 10, 100 and 1000 (no 'answer' cards)?

make up multiplication and division sums using single-digit, two-digit and three-digit numbers (no 'answer' cards)?

make up multiplication and division sums using the numbers 2, 4, 5, 0.8 and 0.5?

level 5

Number Relationships and Operations

Number Facts

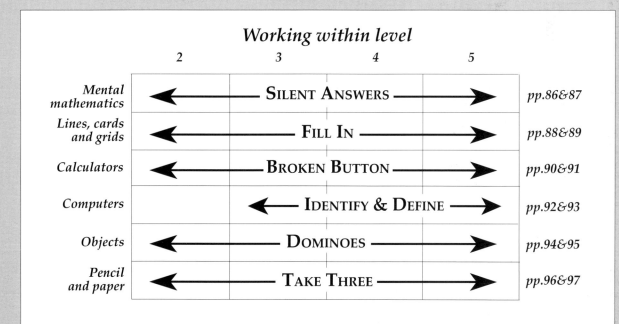

	Working within level				
	2	3	4	5	
Mental mathematics	←	SILENT ANSWERS		→	pp.86&87
Lines, cards and grids	←	FILL IN		→	pp.88&89
Calculators	←	BROKEN BUTTON		→	pp.90&91
Computers		← IDENTIFY & DEFINE		→	pp.92&93
Objects	←	DOMINOES		→	pp.94&95
Pencil and paper	←	TAKE THREE		→	pp.96&97

Silent Answers

Children will experience

- mental practice in all four number operations
- using place value
- thinking flexibly

Equipment

- number cards 0-9 for each child
- number cards 10, 20, 30, . . . (up to 90) for each child — double the width of the other cards
- number cards 100, 200, 300, . . . (up to 900) for each child — three times the width of the other cards

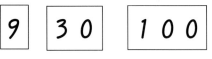

- negative number and decimal point cards

Getting started

This activity can be done with the whole class — although for assessment purposes you will want to focus on just a few children at a time.

Tell the children a number problem and ask them to work out the answer mentally. To avoid children calling out the answers, each child has sets of cards which they use to display the answers. To display two- or three-digit numbers they overlap cards as necessary.

Questions to ask the children

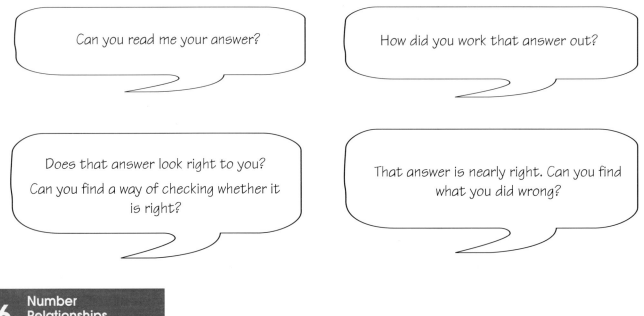

Can you read me your answer?

How did you work that answer out?

Does that answer look right to you?
Can you find a way of checking whether it is right?

That answer is nearly right. Can you find what you did wrong?

Keeping going

◆ Children can work in groups of similar abilities. One child (on a rotating basis) can pose problems for the others to work out, and then check the answers with a calculator. The calculator can be shown silently, and without the others seeing, to anyone who has completed their answer.

Can the children . . .

solve addition and subtraction problems to 10?

display and read numbers accurately to 100?

level 2

---

solve addition and subtraction problems to 100?

solve multiplication and division problems in the 2, 5 and 10 times tables?

solve multiplication and division problems up to 5 x 5?

display and read numbers accurately to 1000?

level 3

---

solve multiplication and division problems up to 10 x 10?

multiply and divide numbers by 10 or 100?

solve one- or two-digit addition and subtraction problems involving decimals?

display and read numbers accurately above 1000?

display and read decimal numbers accurately above 1000?

check the reasonableness of their results?

level 4

---

multiply and divide numbers by 10 or 100 or 1000?

solve two- or three-digit addition and subtraction problems involving negative numbers?

solve simple problems involving decimals, using any of the four operations?

check their results by applying inverse operations?

level 5

FILL IN

Children will experience

◆ practice in mental addition and subtraction
◆ making logical deductions
◆ inverse operations
◆ thinking flexibly

Equipment

◆ squared paper
◆ pencils

Getting started

You can introduce this activity to a group or the whole class.

Show children some addition and subtraction (difference) grids, and help them to make one or two of their own (it is a good idea to stick to consecutive numbers for the row and column headings to begin with). Once they are familiar with the idea of these grids they should make one for a friend, and delete the row or column headings. The task for the friend is to fill in what is missing.

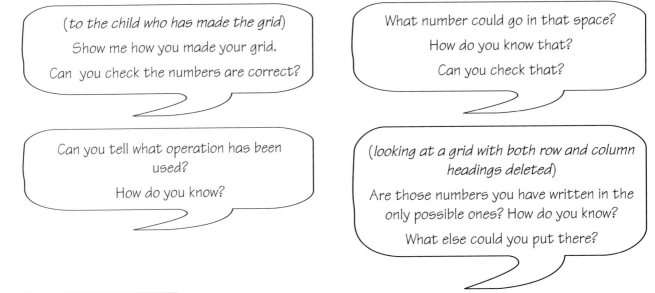

When children are ready to develop this activity further they can explore various alternatives, for example:

— grids using division (hard!) or multiplication

— leaving out row *and* column headings

— using non-consecutive numbers

— leaving the operation box empty

Questions to ask the children

(to the child who has made the grid)
Show me how you made your grid.
Can you check the numbers are correct?

What number could go in that space?
How do you know that?
Can you check that?

Can you tell what operation has been used?
How do you know?

(looking at a grid with both row and column headings deleted)
Are those numbers you have written in the only possible ones? How do you know?
What else could you put there?

Keeping going

◆ Children can put three numbers along the top and/or side.

◆ Children can try filling in only some of the numbers in the matrix.

◆ Children can make grids including negative numbers or fractions or decimals.

◆ Make a matrix like the ones used in the main activity, but completely blank. Make a set of attribute cards showing, for example, 'prime', 'even number', 'over 50'. Put these cards along the top and side of the matrix. Can the children find a card to put in each cell?

Can the children . . .

make an addition or subtraction grid using single-digit numbers?

level 2

make an addition or subtraction grid using two-digit numbers?

fill in missing row or column headings in an addition or subtraction grid using two-digit numbers?

make a multiplication grid using single-digit numbers?

level 3

make a multiplication grid using two-digit numbers?

fill in missing row or column headings in a multiplication grid using one- or two-digit numbers?

check that the grid is correct?

level 4

on a grid with both row and column headings deleted, find all the possible number combinations that could go in the blank spaces?

explain how they know a grid is correct?

level 5

BROKEN BUTTON

Children will experience

◆ practice in all four number operations

◆ thinking flexibly

◆ thinking about equivalent values of number combinations

Equipment

◆ calculators

◆ pencil and paper

Getting started

Give children an addition or subtraction problem to do on the calculator, choosing one that is slightly hard for them and that involves the number 6. They must do it without using the ⑥ button.

Later they can move on to working with multiplication and division problems.

(level 2) The problem might be 6 + 22 = ? which could be solved by pressing, say,
③ ⊞ ③ ⊞ ②② 🟰

(level 3) The problem might be 106 – 26 = ? which could be solved by pressing, say,
①①⓪ ⊟ ③⓪ 🟰

(level 4) The problem might be 162 x 4 = ? which could be solved by pressing, say,
⑧① ⓧ ② ⓧ ④ 🟰

(level 5) The problem might be 63 x 16 = ? which could be solved by pressing, say,
②① ⓧ ③ ⓧ ⑧ ⓧ ② 🟰

Questions to ask the children

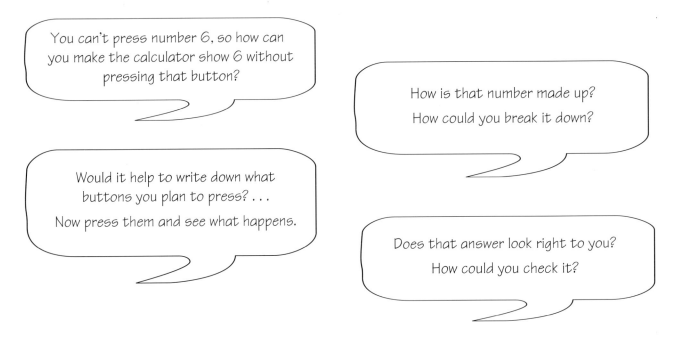

You can't press number 6, so how can you make the calculator show 6 without pressing that button?

How is that number made up?
How could you break it down?

Would it help to write down what buttons you plan to press? . . .
Now press them and see what happens.

Does that answer look right to you?
How could you check it?

Keeping going

◆ Supposing the ⑤ button were broken?

◆ Supposing the ⑥ button *and the* ② *button* were broken?

◆ Supposing all the operation buttons were broken?

◆ Give the children some calculations with the operations missing

(5 • 6) • 4 = 44

9 • 3 • 9 = 12

18 • 18 • 18 = 342

Ask them to use their calculators to work out the missing operations.

Can the children . . .

make the calculator show 6 without pressing that button?

solve a simple addition or subtraction problem such as 6 + 22?

level 2

solve an addition or subtraction problem involving one- or two-digit numbers, such as 66 + 66 or 106 – 26?

check their answers, pressing the number ⑥ if necessary?

level 3

solve a problem involving multiplying single-digit by three-digit numbers? (for example, 162 x 4)

find a way of checking answers without pressing the number ⑥?

level 4

solve a problem involving multiplying or dividing two two-digit numbers? (for example, 63 x 16)

find a way of checking answers without pressing the number ⑥?

level 5

IDENTIFY AND DEFINE

Children will experience
- thinking about the properties of numbers
- thinking logically

Equipment
- software: 'Identify' in *The Next 17* from SMILE
- software: 'Define' in *The Next 17* from SMILE

Getting started

Identify is an activity for a pair or small group where children use their knowledge of number properties to guess a number. The computer produces a set of numbers, and the children try to work out which one the computer is 'thinking of' by asking questions such as 'Is it a square number?'. After each question the computer states 'yes' or 'no' and shows a revised set of numbers containing those that are still possibilities.

Define is an activity for pairs or small groups which provides children with the opportunity to develop logical thinking and use their knowledge of number properties in a problem-solving context. The computer shows a list of numbers and the children use up to six number properties to define one number. The aim is to find the properties which are unique to that number.

Important mathematics to discuss

Children will need to know the meaning of 'factor', 'square number' and 'prime number'.

Children working at level 2 could restrict their questions to, for instance, 'Is it greater than . . ?' or 'Is it a multiple of . . ?'.

Questions to ask the children

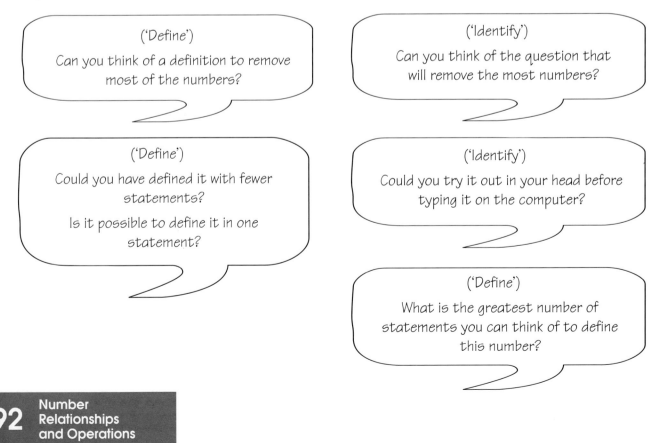

('Define')
Can you think of a definition to remove most of the numbers?

('Identify')
Can you think of the question that will remove the most numbers?

('Define')
Could you have defined it with fewer statements?

Is it possible to define it in one statement?

('Identify')
Could you try it out in your head before typing it on the computer?

('Define')
What is the greatest number of statements you can think of to define this number?

Keeping going

◆ Children can try to think of statements or questions that are not offered on the screen.

◆ Children can play Properties. They each have nine cards bearing a definition statement such as 'multiple of 5' or 'prime'. They take turns to pick a number card and use it to cover a definition card. Whoever covers all nine definition cards first is the winner.

◆ Children can invent a number identification game for the class or for younger children.

◆ Pairs of children can try playing 'Identify' or 'Define' without the computer.

Can the children . . .

not appropriate
level 2

recognise the term 'square number'?
recognise the term 'factor'?
recognise the term 'multiple'?
use multiples of 2, 5 and 10?
level 3

use the terms 'square', 'multiple', 'factor', 'prime number'?
recognise patterns and use these to try out questions mentally?
predict how many steps they will need?
level 4

recognise, understand and use prime numbers?
recognise and express a relationship between the amount of numbers and the number of questions needed?
level 5

DOMINOES

Children will experience

◆ practice in number operations
◆ combining operations
◆ awareness of place value
◆ thinking flexibly

Equipment

◆ sets of dominoes (it doesn't matter whether or not they are complete)
◆ number cards
◆ calculators

Getting started

Children choose two dominoes. They use the number of dots on each half to generate as many number operations as possible. They can use all the numbers or just some of them. For example:

$1 + 3 + 6 + 4 = 14$

$13 \times 64 = 832$

$6 \div 4 = 1.5$

$1 + 3 - 4 = 0$

(At lower levels children could start by exploring the operations to be made from just one domino. For example, the domino 1, 3 could provide $1 + 3 = 4$, $1 \times 3 = 3$ and so on.)

Encourage children to be systematic in looking for all the possible number sentences of a type. For example, if they have used the dominoes above and have written $13 + 64 = 77$, ask them what other number sentences they can make using one half of a domino to represent a 'tens' number. If they then produce $31 + 46 = 77$, ask them "Can you find any more like that? Can you find *all* the sums like that?".

Questions to ask the children

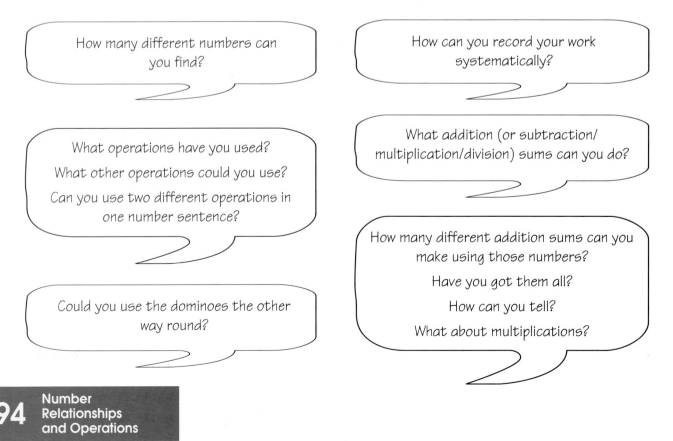

How many different numbers can you find?

How can you record your work systematically?

What operations have you used?

What other operations could you use?

Can you use two different operations in one number sentence?

What addition (or subtraction/ multiplication/division) sums can you do?

How many different addition sums can you make using those numbers?

Have you got them all?

How can you tell?

What about multiplications?

Could you use the dominoes the other way round?

Keeping going

◆ Get children to work in pairs and when they have both finished to check each other's work.

◆ Children can explore all the possible sums using two dominoes and just one operation.

◆ Ask children: "What numbers under 100 *can't* you make with those two dominoes?"

◆ Children can use decimal numbers as well as whole numbers — or *only* decimal numbers.

◆ Children can try to find answers that fit a certain category — over 10, decimal numbers, negative numbers.

◆ Children can work with three dominoes.

◆ *Domino Challenge*
Children make up challenges for each other — for example "Make the highest number possible using any two dominoes".

Can the children . . .

<table>
<tr><td>

add the two halves of a domino, then find other dominoes whose halves add up to the same amount?

find the difference between the two halves of a domino, then find other dominoes whose halves have the same difference?

record their work?

level 2

</td><td>

choose two dominoes and add the four numbers together?

find other domino pairs whose numbers add up to the same amount?

record their work?

level 3

</td></tr>
<tr><td>

find all the possible number problems using two dominoes and just one operation?

justify their statement that they have found all the possibilities?

level 4

</td><td>

make up number problems using a decimal point correctly? (for example, given these two dominoes, write 1.4 + 6.1 = 7.5)

level 5

</td></tr>
</table>

TAKE THREE

Children will experience

◆ mental practice in all four
  number operations
◆ combining operations
◆ thinking flexibly

Equipment

◆ paper and pencil
◆ three-minute timer or stopwatch
◆ calculator (optional)

Getting started

This activity can be done with the whole class or a group in any convenient time-slot of
about 15 minutes.

Each child needs a sheet of paper and a pen or pencil. Give
them a single-digit number to write in the middle of their
sheet (for example, 5), and ask them to write down as
many equations as they can with that number as the
answer, in just three minutes. At the end of this time they
must put their pencils down.

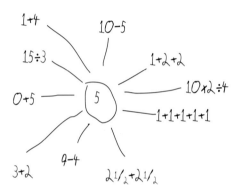

If this is a whole-class activity, you could collect up all the
different answers on a large sheet of paper, or blackboard,
and perhaps involve the class in sorting them. If it is a
group activity, children could swap sheets and check each
other's.

Questions to ask the children

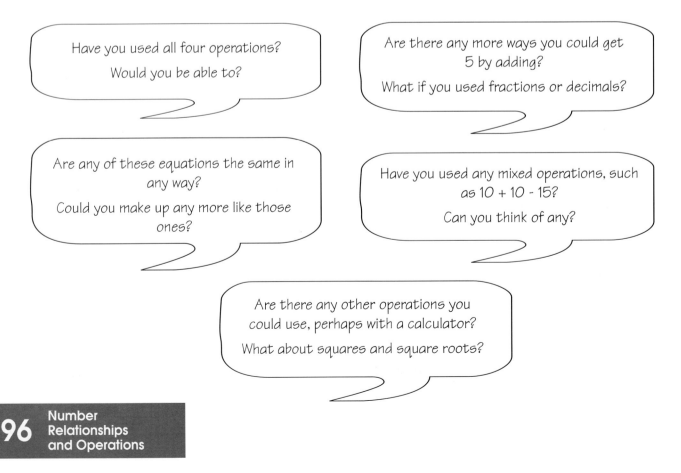

Have you used all four operations?
Would you be able to?

Are there any more ways you could get
5 by adding?
What if you used fractions or decimals?

Are any of these equations the same in
any way?
Could you make up any more like those
ones?

Have you used any mixed operations, such
as 10 + 10 - 15?
Can you think of any?

Are there any other operations you
could use, perhaps with a calculator?
What about squares and square roots?

Keeping going

◆ With younger or less able children you may prefer to give them 5 or even 10 minutes.

◆ Give the children a different single-digit number, or a higher number such as 10, 24, 50 or 100.

◆ Give the children 0 as the answer.

◆ Children can explore 'as many ways as possible' of making their number — with no time limit.

◆ This activity can be turned into a game for a group of children: at the end of the three minutes, any equations which more than one person has written down are crossed out. Whoever has most 'unique' equations is the winner.

Can the children . . .

use addition and subtraction to make equations up to 10?

level 2

use addition and subtraction to make equations up to 20 or higher?

use multiplication and division to make equations in the 2, 5 or 10 multiplication tables?

use multiplication and division to make equations up to 5 x 5?

use mixed operations? (for example, 10 + 10 – 15)

level 3

use addition and subtraction of whole numbers to make equations up to 100 or higher?

use addition and subtraction of decimal numbers to make equations?

use multiplication and division to make equations up to 10 x 10?

show systematic ways of working?

level 4

use addition and subtraction of decimal numbers and fractions to make equations?

explain that there is an infinite number of possible answers, and why this is so?

level 5

Solving Numerical Problems

Checking, Estimating and Approximating

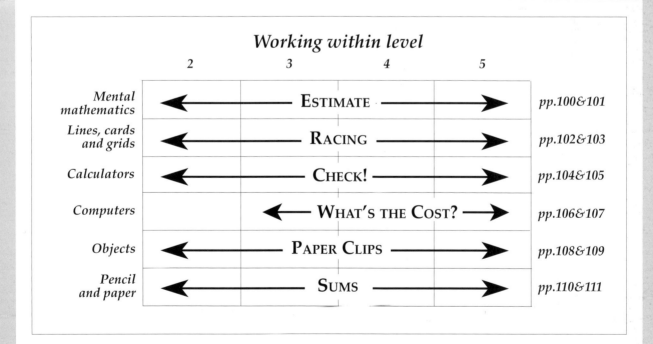

ESTIMATE

Children will experience
- developing strategies for estimation
- mental calculation
- finding differences

Equipment
- calculators
- paper and pencil
- number cards 0-10 (level 2)
- number cards 0-100 (levels 3-5)

Getting started

Children work in pairs, sharing a sheet of paper. Each child picks a number card and writes down the number. They then work together to estimate the result of adding, subtracting, multiplying and dividing (both ways) those two numbers, and write down their estimates.

They then do the calculations on the calculator, compare their results with their estimates, and find the difference between their estimates and the actual calculation.

As children continue working with other pairs of numbers, they should aim to lessen the gap between their estimates and the real answer.

17 and 39

	estimate	answer	difference
+	56	56	0
−	22	22	0
×	500	663	163
÷	2	2.29	0.29
or	.5	0.43	0.06

Questions to ask the children

How did you work out your estimate for that operation?

Do you think it worked well? Would you use it again?

What might you round that number up to? And that one?

So roughly how big would the answer be if you added them?

How close was your estimate for the multiplication one?

Are you getting better at estimating multiplications?

Approximately how big will the answer be when you multiply those two numbers?

What is a good way of getting an answer that is close?

You've divided that number by that one. What happens when you swap them around?

Which ones were easy to do and which weren't?

Which ones did you work out and which did you estimate?

Keeping going

◆ Children can work with just addition and subtraction using higher numbers.

◆ Children can concentrate on division, using single-digit numbers.

◆ Give children real problems where there is a need to estimate and approximate: How much bread will we need to make sandwiches for the party? How much 'roofing tile' wallpaper will we need to buy for the dolls' house roof?

◆ Some children will be able to work with numbers over 100.

◆ Children can work with three numbers, just adding and multiplying.

11 and 40 and 15

	estimate	answer	difference
+	66	66	0
×	6000	6600	600

Can the children . . .

make sensible estimates of some multiplication problems using single-digit numbers?

make sensible estimates of addition and subtraction problems using two-digit numbers?

level 2

---

give the exact answer for multiplication and division problems in the 2, 5 or 10 times tables?

make sensible estimates of other multiplication problems using single-digit numbers?

make sensible estimates of some division problems?

make sensible estimates of — or calculate mentally — addition and subtraction problems using two-digit numbers?

level 3

---

give the exact answer for multiplication and division problems in any of the times tables?

make sensible estimates of multiplication and division problems using two-digit numbers?

level 4

---

make sensible estimates of division problems using single- or two-digit numbers?

make sensible estimates of — or calculate mentally — addition and subtraction problems using three-digit numbers?

level 5

RACING

Children will experience

◆ rounding whole numbers up and down
◆ rounding decimal numbers up and down
◆ estimating

Equipment

◆ counters
◆ ordinary dice
◆ dice numbered 1, 1.5, 2, 2.5, 3, 3.5
◆ blank dice
◆ felt-tipped pens
◆ 0-100 or other number lines
◆ 100-squares or other number squares

Getting started

This activity is for groups of 2 or 3 children. The children take turns to toss dice, round the number up or down, and move that many steps along the number line or track. It can be played at different levels and with different equipment. For example:

(level 2) toss two dice and find the total, round the number to the nearest 0 or 5 (or 10), and move a counter along a 1-100 number square (or draw jumps on a 0-100 number line) — when you get to 100 turn round and head back to 0

(level 3) toss two dice and find the difference, round the number to the nearest 0 or 5, and move a counter along a 1-100 number square or draw jumps on a 0-100 number line

(level 4) toss two dice and multiply the numbers together, round the number to the nearest 10, and move a counter along a 10-1000 number square (numbered 10, 20, 30, . . .) or draw jumps on a 0-1000 number line (numbered 0, 10, 20, 30, . . .)

(level 5) toss two dice and divide one number by the other, round the number to the nearest 1, and move a counter along a 1-100 number square or draw jumps on a 0-50 number line (children working at this level may prefer to keep a score rather than moving counters)

Questions to ask the children

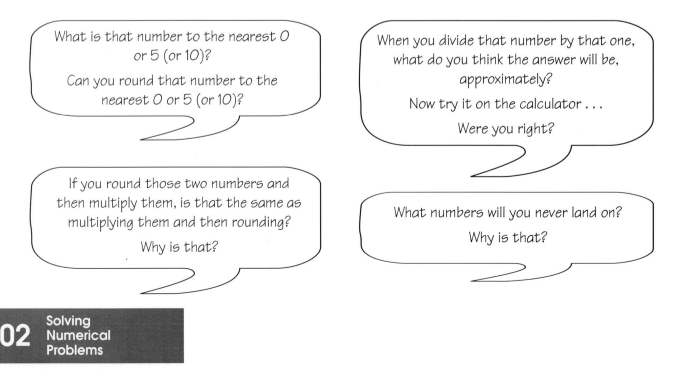

What is that number to the nearest 0 or 5 (or 10)?

Can you round that number to the nearest 0 or 5 (or 10)?

When you divide that number by that one, what do you think the answer will be, approximately?

Now try it on the calculator . . .

Were you right?

If you round those two numbers and then multiply them, is that the same as multiplying them and then rounding?

Why is that?

What numbers will you never land on?

Why is that?

Keeping going

◆ Children can make their own number tracks for these games, perhaps highlighting the numbers that it is possible to land on in their particular version.

◆ Instead of moving counters along a line or track, children can accumulate base ten blocks.

◆ Ask children to keep a record of their dice-throws and what the number rounded up or down to.

◆ Children can explore rounding up and down by working with a supermarket check-out receipt. Ask them to round each item to the nearest pound and compare their answer with the actual total. How far out is it? Does the discrepancy vary much from bill to bill?

Can the children . . .

use two 1-6 dice, add or subtract the numbers, and round the numbers to the nearest 5 or 10?

play the game on a number line or track going from 0 (or 1) to 100 and then back again to 0 (or 1)?

level 2

when working with whole and decimal numbers such as 2, 2.5, 3, 3.5, round the total to the nearest whole number?

when working with whole and fractional numbers such as 2, $2\frac{1}{4}$, $3\frac{1}{2}$, $4\frac{3}{4}$, round the total to the nearest whole number?

level 3

when multiplying whole and decimal numbers such as 2, 2.5, 3, 3.5, round the total to the nearest whole number, or 10?

play the game on a 0-1000 line or a 1-1000 track numbered in tens?

level 4

when dividing whole numbers, round the total to the nearest whole number?

round any number to one decimal place?

play the game on a decimal line numbered in tenths?

level 5

CHECK!

Children will experience
◆ practice in checking calculations
◆ using inverse operations

Equipment
◆ calculators
◆ pencils and paper

Getting started

This activity involves children in writing number sentences and sometimes deliberately putting the wrong answer. Their partner must catch them out by checking the operation using a different method.

Children work in pairs.

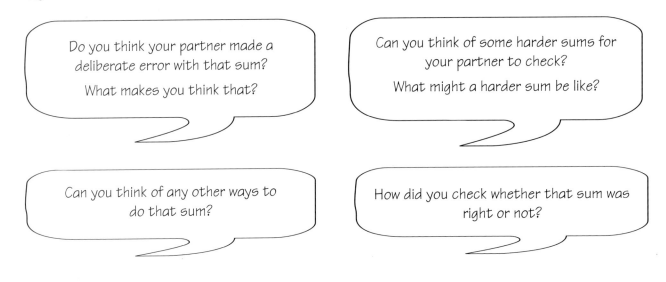

sum	right/wrong	how I know
30 + 11 = 41	yes	41 − 11 = 30
25 + 63 = 88	yes	20 + 60 + 5 + 3 = 88
78 + 29 = 106	no	If I add the 8 and 9 the answer should end in 7

● Each child chooses two two-digit numbers and uses them to write down an addition sum (using a calculator if necessary)

● They work out the answer and write it down — or deliberately get the answer slightly wrong

● The children then swap, and each checks the other's answer (without the aid of a calculator) by using a method other than a straight addition (for instance they could use the inverse operation, or break the sum down into smaller elements)

As children become confident with the activity they should move on to larger numbers and the other operations. Many division sums will involve decimal numbers, sometimes with a long string of digits after the decimal point. The children will need to make decisions about when and how to round these numbers up or down.

Questions to ask the children

Do you think your partner made a deliberate error with that sum?

What makes you think that?

Can you think of some harder sums for your partner to check?

What might a harder sum be like?

Can you think of any other ways to do that sum?

How did you check whether that sum was right or not?

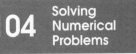

Checking, Estimating and Approximating: Pencil and Paper

Keeping going

◆ Children check the answers *only* by doing the inverse operation.

◆ Children choose two numbers and use them to write four calculations using each of the four operations (addition, subtraction, multiplication and division).

$$23 + 59 = 82 \qquad 59 - 23 = 36$$
$$23 \times 59 = 1357 \qquad 23 \div 59 = 0.3898$$

◆ This activity links well with *Breaking Down* on page 124.

◆ Ask children to invent some problems in context (involving approximation, estimation and rounding) for each other to solve.

About how many sheets of paper does the class use in a week?

Can the children . . .

<table>
<tr>
<td>

add one- and two-digit numbers using a calculator?

level 2
</td>
<td>

add and subtract two-digit numbers, using a calculator where necessary?

check answers by using the inverse operation, or by breaking the sum down into its elements? (for example, $72 - 9 = 70 + 2 - 9 = 61 + ? = 63$)

level 3
</td>
</tr>
<tr>
<td>

add and subtract two- and three-digit numbers?

multiply and divide one- and two-digit numbers, using a calculator where necessary?

use a variety of strategies for checking and assessing answers? (for example, to check $7 \times 15 = 100$, say "It's the same as 70 and 35. That's more than 100")

level 4
</td>
<td>

multiply and divide two- and three-digit numbers, using a calculator where necessary?

use a variety of strategies for checking and assessing answers? (for example, to check $75 \times 45 = 3375$, say "The answer should be between 80×50, that's 4000, and 70×40, that's 2800, and it is, so it could be right")

level 5
</td>
</tr>
</table>

WHAT'S THE COST?

Children will experience

◆ rounding numbers
◆ working with approximations
◆ checking the plausibility of answers

Equipment

◆ any spreadsheet program
◆ measuring cylinders
◆ bottles and cartons of milk with price labels
◆ bottles and cartons of other liquids with price labels (try to provide different-sized containers of the same liquid)
◆ calculators

Getting started

Children will need to have used spreadsheets before. (The activity on page 36 is useful as an introduction.)

Ask the children to estimate how much 100 ml of milk (or another drink) costs. They should then use a spreadsheet to work it out. If children want help setting up the spreadsheet, suggest they use the following columns:

cost of carton	volume in ml	cost per 1 ml	cost per 100 ml

They can go on to explore 'best buys' — which container of a particular liquid (drink, shampoo, washing-up liquid . . .) gives best value for money?

Questions to ask the children

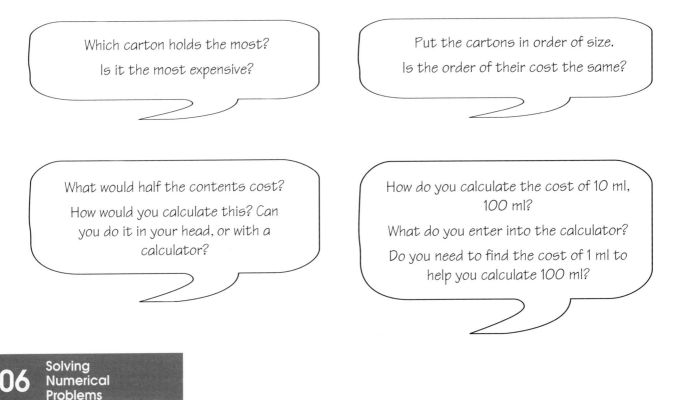

Which carton holds the most?

Is it the most expensive?

Put the cartons in order of size.

Is the order of their cost the same?

What would half the contents cost?

How would you calculate this? Can you do it in your head, or with a calculator?

How do you calculate the cost of 10 ml, 100 ml?

What do you enter into the calculator?

Do you need to find the cost of 1 ml to help you calculate 100 ml?

Keeping going

◆ Children can use this method to compare costs for all kinds of grocery: crisps, biscuits, sweets, apples, nuts . . .

Can the children . . .

not appropriate
level 2

use their understanding of place value to order the contents and prices of the items?
use decimal notation in money?
mentally recall facts from the 2, 5 and 10 mutiplication tables?
use calculator methods to solve problems?
level 3

use their understanding of place value to multiply and divide by 10 and 100?
use mental methods to solve problems?
mentally recall facts up to 10 x 10?
level 4

use their understanding of place value to multiply and divide by 10, 100 and 1000?
calculate with decimals to two decimal places?
calculate fractional parts of quantities using both a calculator and non-calculator method?
check their solutions?
level 5

Paper Clips

Children will experience

- counting accurately
- counting in twos, fives, tens or twenties
- working with addition and multiplication
- estimating quantities and improving estimation skills

Equipment

- small objects such as paper clips, acorns, dried peas or beads
- one-, two- and five-minute timers
- measuring equipment such as scales and measuring cylinders

Getting started

This activity is for pairs of children. You can introduce it to a group or the whole class before splitting the children up.

Each pair needs a container filled with small objects such as paper clips, acorns or beads — somewhere between 50 and 1000. Ask them to find out approximately how many of their object there are, but tell them they have only got two minutes (or five, depending on which you think appropriate) to do it in, so their answer can only be approximate.

When their time is up they should write down their approximate answer. They can then take as long as they need to count the objects accurately. Encourage them to assess their estimate and how close it was.

Questions to ask the children

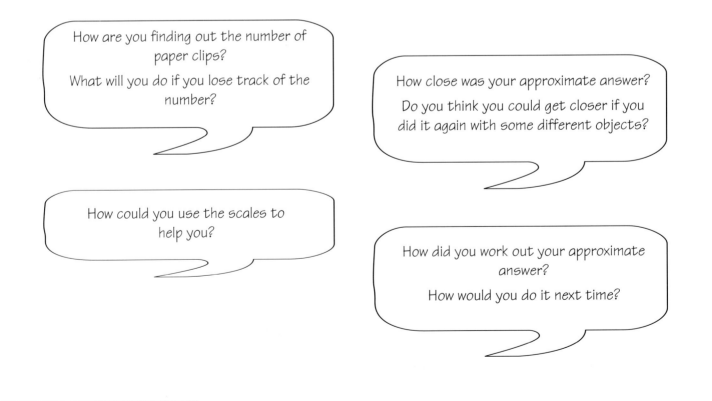

How are you finding out the number of paper clips?

What will you do if you lose track of the number?

How close was your approximate answer?

Do you think you could get closer if you did it again with some different objects?

How could you use the scales to help you?

How did you work out your approximate answer?

How would you do it next time?

Keeping going

◆ Younger children can count, say, 20 paper clips into each compartment of an egg box to help them keep track of their work.

◆ Give children the same kind of object for their next count, but in a different quantity.

◆ Pairs can swap their containers of objects with each other in order to try again with a different object to count.

◆ Give children a mixture of two kinds of object — for example, conkers and dried peas.

◆ Make the activity into a game by inventing a scoring system — or asking children to. The closer the estimate the higher the score.

Can the children . . .

make a sensible estimate of about 100 objects?
talk about how they made their estimate?
count the objects accurately?
compare their estimate with the actual count and work out how far out they were?
level 2

make a sensible estimate of up to 1000 objects?
talk about how they made their estimate?
count the objects accurately?
compare their estimate with the actual count and work out how far out they were?
level 3

use more than one strategy for estimating?
level 4

use strategies such as measuring the weight or volume of ten objects, and then all of them together, in order to reach a close approximation?
level 5

SUMS

Children will experience
- making quick approximations to a calculation
- calculating mentally

Equipment
- pencils and paper
- calculators
- timers

Getting started

Children work in pairs. Each child writes down a list of five numbers (under 100 for younger children, over 100 for older ones) and they then swap lists.

The next part of the activity should be done quickly — perhaps to a time limit. The partner quickly writes down three operations whose answer is that number. If possible, an answer should be accurate; if not, it should come close to it.

They then swap lists back, and the first child uses a calculator to check their partner's calculations and to work out their score.

Children can use the following scoring system, or make up their own.

		score for accuracy		score for calculation	total
12	10+2	✓	2	0	2
	5+7	✓	2	0	2
	2×6	✓	2	2	4
70	30+40	✓	2	0	2
	100−20	✗	0	0	0
	69+1	✓	2	0	2
78	77+1	✓	2	0	2
	8×9	✗	0	2	2
	79−1	✓	2	1	3
32	30+2	✓	2	0	2
	40−7	✗	0	1	1
	64÷2	✓	2	3	5
59	50+9	✓	2	0	2
	60−1	✓	2	1	3
	58.5+0.5	✓	2	4	6

Scoring	Points
Each correct calculation:	2
In addition, for calculations that are either correct or within 10 of being correct:	1 for a subtraction, 2 for a multiplication, 3 for a division, 4 for using decimals or fractions

Questions to ask the children

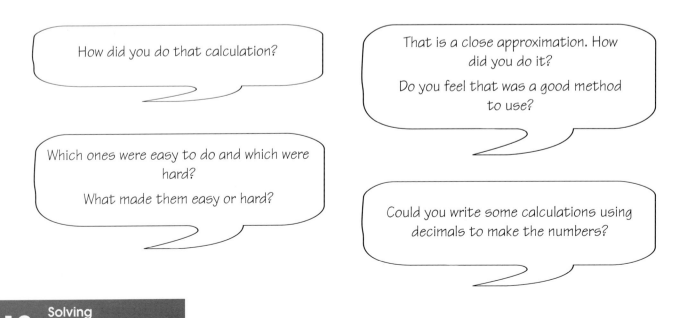

How did you do that calculation?

That is a close approximation. How did you do it?

Do you feel that was a good method to use?

Which ones were easy to do and which were hard?

What made them easy or hard?

Could you write some calculations using decimals to make the numbers?

Keeping going

◆ To ensure children use a variety of operations, add this rule: in the first round they must all be additions, in the next they must all be subtractions, and in the third multiplications or divisions. These last might need to be two-stage operations such as:

$$3 \times 15 + 4 = 49$$

◆ Children can work with negative or decimal numbers.

◆ Children producing two-stage operations score extra points. For example:

$$2 \times 12 - 4 = 20$$

Can the children . . .

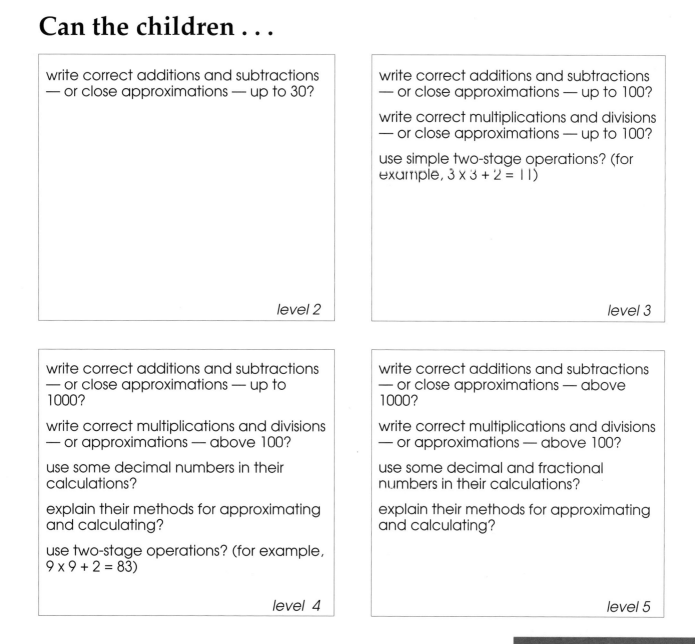

write correct additions and subtractions — or close approximations — up to 30?

level 2

write correct additions and subtractions — or close approximations — up to 100?

write correct multiplications and divisions — or close approximations — up to 100?

use simple two-stage operations? (for example, $3 \times 3 + 2 = 11$)

level 3

write correct additions and subtractions — or close approximations — up to 1000?

write correct multiplications and divisions — or approximations — above 100?

use some decimal numbers in their calculations?

explain their methods for approximating and calculating?

use two-stage operations? (for example, $9 \times 9 + 2 = 83$)

level 4

write correct additions and subtractions — or close approximations — above 1000?

write correct multiplications and divisions — or approximations — above 100?

use some decimal and fractional numbers in their calculations?

explain their methods for approximating and calculating?

level 5

Relationships Between Operations

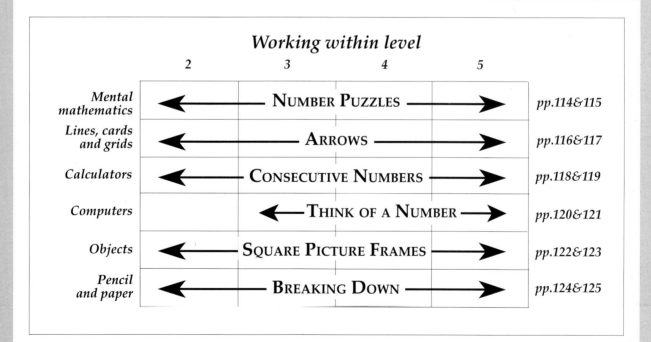

NUMBER PUZZLES

Children will experience
◆ exploring the relationships between operations
◆ developing problem-solving strategies

Equipment
◆ pencil and paper
◆ calculator

Getting started

Present children with one of the following puzzles, and get them to explore it for a number of their choice. Ask them to consider "Does it work for any number?".

What's My Number?

(level 2)

I'm thinking of a number.
I double it and I get 12.
What's my number?

(level 3)

I'm thinking of a number.
I add 3 to it.
I double the answer.
I get 14.
What's my number?

Back to Your Original Number

(levels 3/4)

Think of a number.
Add 3.
Multiply by 2.
Subtract 6.
Halve the answer.
You are back to your original answer.

The Answer is 2

(levels 4/5)

Think of a number.
Add 3.
Double it.
Take away your first number.
Take away 4.
Take away your first number.
Your answer is 2.

Questions to ask the children

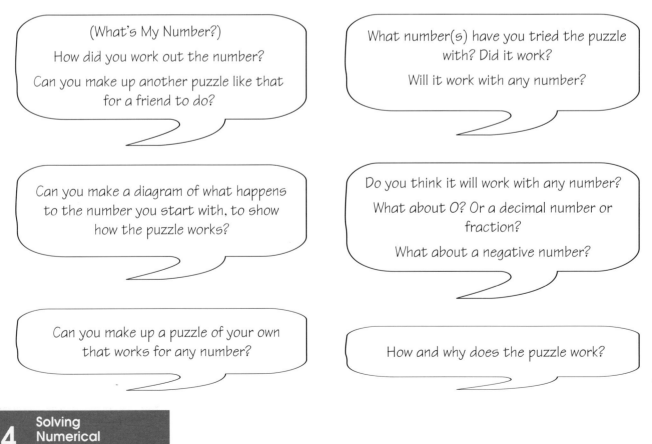

(What's My Number?)
How did you work out the number?
Can you make up another puzzle like that for a friend to do?

What number(s) have you tried the puzzle with? Did it work?
Will it work with any number?

Can you make a diagram of what happens to the number you start with, to show how the puzzle works?

Do you think it will work with any number?
What about 0? Or a decimal number or fraction?
What about a negative number?

Can you make up a puzzle of your own that works for any number?

How and why does the puzzle work?

Keeping going

◆ This activity fits very well with the next one, 'Arrows'.

◆ It is a good idea for children to make up their own puzzles as this helps them understand how they are constructed and how they 'work'.

◆ Children can make flow charts to show the path of a number 'through the puzzle'.

◆ Ask children 'Can you change the problem or add another stage to it without changing the result? What happens when you try?'

◆ A spreadsheet version of this activity appears on pages 120 and 121.

◆ Children can record their results in tabular form.

No.	+3	×2	−6	1/2
10	13	26	20	10
3	6	12	6	3
19	22	44	38	19

Can the children . . .

---

solve one-stage 'What's My Number?' puzzles involving addition or subtraction of single-digit numbers?

explain how they worked out the number?

make up a similar puzzle for a friend to do?

level 2

---

solve two-stage 'What's My Number?' puzzles, by trial and improvement if necessary?

make up a similar puzzle?

undo one step of a 'What's My Number?' puzzle by using the inverse operation and explain what they are doing?

level 3

---

solve 'What's My Number?' or 'Back to Your Original Number' puzzles by using the inverse operations?

explain what they are doing?

draw diagrams to show the path of a number 'through the puzzle'?

make up similar puzzles that work for any number?

explore whether the puzzles work for 0?

level 4

---

solve 'The Answer is 2' type puzzles by using the inverse operations?

explain what they are doing and why the sequence 'works'?

make up similar puzzles that work for any number?

explore whether these and other puzzles work for negative numbers?

explore whether these and other puzzles work for decimal numbers and fractions?

level 5

ARROWS

Children will experience

◆ exploring the relationships between operations
◆ generalising

Equipment

◆ 0-9 number cards
◆ spare blank cards
◆ a set of arrow cards with an operation and number on one side — they should be blank on the reverse
◆ spare blank arrow cards
◆ calculators
◆ 1-100 square

Getting started

Arrange two number cards and an arrow card to form a number sentence such as 5 + 3 = 8.

Now reverse the direction of the arrow card, by flipping it over, and ask the children what number operation belongs on the other side of the arrow. Ask them to make various number sentences, reverse the arrow each time, and explore the results.

When children are confident that the reverse side of an arrow always represents the same inverse operation, they can write that operation on it.

As children explore this activity encourage them to try more challenging number sentences.

(*levels 3 and 4*)   reversing multiple addition and subtraction operations, such as
3 + 14 − 2 = 15

(*levels 5 and 6*)   reversing multiple operations involving brackets, such as
(5 + 25) x 3 = 90

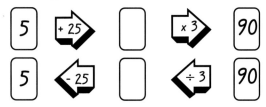

Questions to ask the children

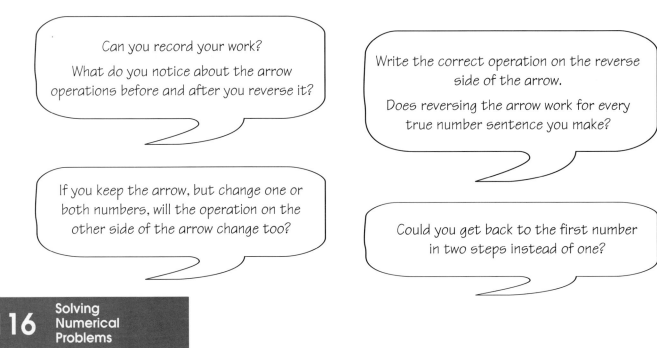

Can you record your work?

What do you notice about the arrow operations before and after you reverse it?

Write the correct operation on the reverse side of the arrow.

Does reversing the arrow work for every true number sentence you make?

If you keep the arrow, but change one or both numbers, will the operation on the other side of the arrow change too?

Could you get back to the first number in two steps instead of one?

Keeping going

◆ This activity fits very well with the previous one, 'Number Puzzles'.

◆ Younger children may enjoy making flipping arrows: they cut out an arrow shape and write an operation on it, then tape it to a sheet of paper by its 'tail'. They use this to explore various number sentences and their opposites. Once the children are convinced about what belongs on the reverse of the arrow they can write it on it.

Can the children . . .

<table>
<tr><td>

arrange two number cards and an arrow card to form a number sentence such as 5 + 3 = 8?

reverse the arrow and say what operation it now represents?

level 2
</td><td>

arrange number and arrow cards to form multiple operations involving addition and subtraction, such as 3 + 14 – 2 = 15?

reverse the arrows and say what operations they now represent?

explain that the reverse of an arrow always represents the same operation?

level 3
</td></tr>
<tr><td>

make and reverse number multiple operations involving addition and subtraction, such as 3 + 5 + 25 = 33?

reverse the arrows and say what operations they now represent?

explain their work?

level 4
</td><td>

make and reverse operations with decimal numbers involving addition and subtraction, such as 2 + 0.5 + 1.5 = 4?

make and reverse multiple operations involving any of the four operations, such as 3 x (5 + 25) = 90?

make general number statements about these operations, such as "You undo the last calculation first and do them all backwards, in order"?

level 5
</td></tr>
</table>

CONSECUTIVE NUMBERS

Children will experience
◆ exploring the relationships between various operations
◆ developing problem-solving strategies
◆ using trial and improvement methods

Equipment
◆ calculators
◆ pencil and paper

Getting started

Children should work in pairs of roughly equal ability. Each child adds two consecutive numbers, and gives the total to their partner who must work out the original numbers.

When they are familiar with this some children can go on to:

— adding three or more consecutive numbers, or

— multiplying two consecutive numbers

Questions to ask the children

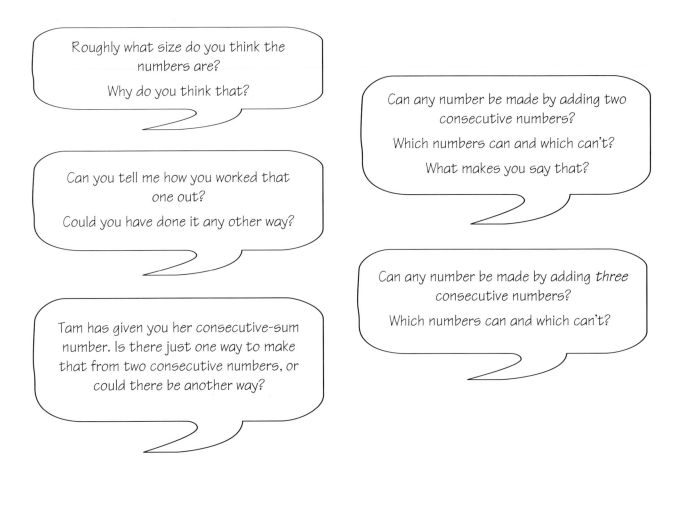

Roughly what size do you think the numbers are?

Why do you think that?

Can you tell me how you worked that one out?

Could you have done it any other way?

Tam has given you her consecutive-sum number. Is there just one way to make that from two consecutive numbers, or could there be another way?

Can any number be made by adding two consecutive numbers?

Which numbers can and which can't?

What makes you say that?

Can any number be made by adding *three* consecutive numbers?

Which numbers can and which can't?

Keeping going

◆ Children can work in fours, with each pair setting a problem for the other pair. This encourages discussion of strategies.

◆ One child can set a problem for a group to work on as individuals. When everyone has solved it, the children can share strategies.

◆ As they begin to set each other slightly harder problems, children can give each other clues — "I've added two consecutive numbers to make 155. There are three sevens in the answer".

Can the children . . .

understand what consecutive numbers are?

using a calculator if necessary, work out which two consecutive numbers were added to make a total under 20?

level 2

work out which two consecutive numbers were added to make a total under 100?

work out whether any number can be made by adding two consecutive numbers?

explain their method of working out the answer to a problem?

level 3

work out which three consecutive numbers were added to make a given total?

say whether there is just one way to make a number by adding two consecutive numbers, and explain their reasoning?

explain their method of working out the answer to a problem?

make generalisations about adding odd and even numbers, such as "Adding an odd and an even number always gives you an odd answer"?

level 4

work out which two consecutive numbers were multiplied together to make a given total?

say whether there is just one way to make a number by multiplying two consecutive numbers, and explain their reasoning?

explain their method of working out the answer to a problem?

make generalisations about the effect of multiplying odd and even numbers?

level 5

THINK OF A NUMBER

Children will experience
◆ exploring the relationships between operations
◆ developing problem-solving strategies
◆ developing spreadsheet skills

Equipment
◆ pencil and paper
◆ calculator
◆ any spreadsheet program

Getting started

Children should already have worked with one or more of the puzzles from page 114. Now encourage them to use a spreadsheet to explore such puzzles with numbers of their choice.

I'm thinking of a number.
I add 3 to it.
I double the answer.
I get 14.
What's my number?

number	add 2	x 3
6	8	24
2	4	12
10	12	36
1.5	3.5	10.5
0.1	2.1	6.3

Encourage the children to predict what will happen to each number: "If I put in 20 it will turn into 66".

They can also make up their own number puzzles, and set each other challenges: "I'm hiding the first column. Can you look at the other columns and tell me all the numbers I've hidden?"

Questions to ask the children

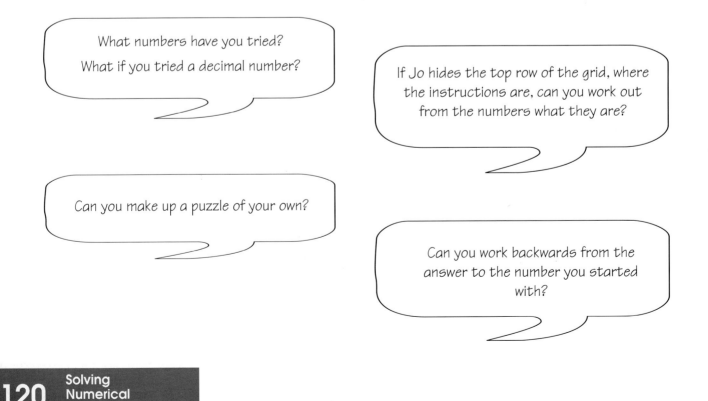

What numbers have you tried?
What if you tried a decimal number?

If Jo hides the top row of the grid, where the instructions are, can you work out from the numbers what they are?

Can you make up a puzzle of your own?

Can you work backwards from the answer to the number you started with?

Keeping going

◆ Encourage children to explore the other puzzles from page 114 — and any others that they find in number puzzle books.

◆ Ask children "Can you change the problem or add another stage to it?"

Can the children . . .

<table>
<tr>
<td>

not appropriate

level 2
</td>
<td>

analyse simple puzzles on a spreadsheet?

talk about what is happening on a prepared spreadsheet?

enter more numbers on a prepared spreadsheet and begin to make predictions?

level 3
</td>
</tr>
<tr>
<td>

make up similar puzzles using a spreadsheet?

talk about what is happening on their spreadsheet?

explore whether these and other puzzles work for decimal numbers?

level 4
</td>
<td>

explore whether these puzzles work for negative numbers?

explore whether these and other puzzles work for decimal numbers?

say that multiplication and division are inverses?

say that the order in which you use addition and subtraction does not affect the answer, whereas with multiplication and division it does?

level 5
</td>
</tr>
</table>

SQUARE PICTURE FRAMES

Children will experience

♦ exploring number patterns involving addition and multiplication

♦ generalising

Equipment

♦ Cuisenaire rods or linking cubes

♦ squared paper

♦ small plastic or card tiles

Getting started

You can introduce this activity to a group or the whole class.

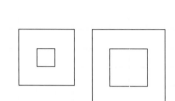

Explain to children that for this activity a 'picture frame' is a square enclosure made from linking cubes or drawn on paper. Ask them to make a series of 'picture frames' of increasing size, starting with the smallest, which will frame a single square. They should record the length of each frame as well as the number of cubes (or squares) used in its construction and the area enclosed. What patterns can they discover?

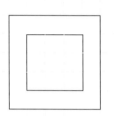

An easier investigation for children working within level 2 involves seeing how oblong picture frames grow if the height is kept the same but the length is increased.

Questions to ask the children

Are your frames a series?

Can you put them in order?

Are any missing?

What patterns can you see in those numbers?

Can you make a rule to describe what is happening?

How do the lengths increase?

What about the number of cubes in the frame?

And the area enclosed?

How many cubes would you need for the next picture frame in the series?

How do you work it out?

Can you tell me how your picture frame is growing?

And what about the size of the picture inside?

How many cubes would you need for the 6th picture frame in the series?

The 10th? The 50th?

Keeping going

◆ Another investigation is exploring the way that the perimeter grows as the picture frame does — perhaps children could think of it in terms of the amount of beading needed to fit round the edge of the picture frames.

◆ Children can investigate picture frames of other shapes. For instance, they can use isometric paper to explore triangular frames; or squared paper to investigate L-shaped frames.

Can the children . . .

work with an oblong frame whose height is kept constant but whose length increases?

put their frames in order and say if any are missing?

say how many cubes would be needed for the next picture frame in the series?

explain that the number of cubes in the frames increases by two each time?

level 2

work with a square frame whose height and length increases?

put their frames in order and say if any are missing?

say how many cubes would be needed for the next picture frame in the series?

explain that the number of cubes in the frames increases by four each time?

level 3

explain why the number of cubes in the frames increases by four each time?

explain that the area enclosed is always a square number?

give a rule for the number of cubes needed for the frame each time?

give a rule for how the area enclosed increases each time?

explore other 'picture frames' and explain their patterns?

level 4

write a formula to describe the number of cubes needed for any frame? (for example, 'It's 2l + 2, where l is the length')

work out how many cubes would be needed for any picture frame in the series?

explore other 'picture frames' and make rules to describe their patterns?

level 5

BREAKING DOWN

Children will experience

◆ using the relationships between operations
◆ thinking about equivalent numbers and operations
◆ developing problem-solving strategies

Equipment

◆ pencil and paper
◆ base ten blocks or linking cubes (for levels 2 and 3)
◆ calculator

Getting started

Give children a written sum that is just a bit hard for them to work out mentally. Ask them to break the sum down into parts so that they can solve it. Typical sums might be:

(*level 2*)   16 + 7; 21 − 4

(*level 3*)   16 x 4; 150 + 135

(*level 4*)   16 x 17; 1197 − 563; 5 x (34 + 79)

(*level 5*)   164 x 7; 48 x 1.5; 15 x (94 − 79)

At first, younger children may find it helpful to model their sums with base ten blocks or cubes, and see how they can rearrange the numbers to make a sum they *can* do. They should, however, aim to develop their skills at this work so that they can visualise the numbers without modelling them.

Children can use a calculator to check their answers. If they are wrong, encourage them to look and see if they can find their error and put it right.

16 x 4
16 x 4 is the same as
10 x 4 and 6 x 4

10 x 4 = 40
6 x 4 = 6+6+6+6 = 24

so 16 x 4 = 40 + 24
which is 64

Questions to ask the children

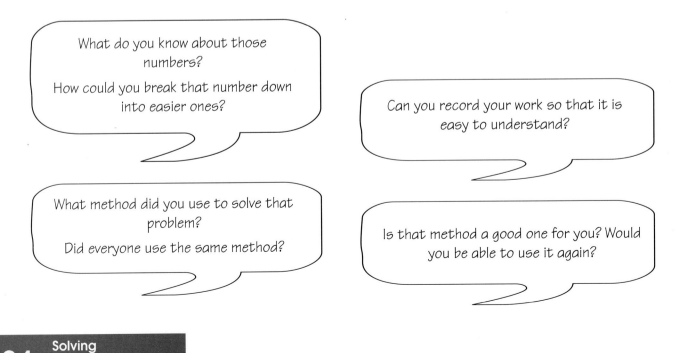

What do you know about those numbers?

How could you break that number down into easier ones?

Can you record your work so that it is easy to understand?

What method did you use to solve that problem?

Did everyone use the same method?

Is that method a good one for you? Would you be able to use it again?

Keeping going

◆ Children can work in pairs, setting each other problems to tackle.

Can the children . . .

work out addition and subtraction problems involving a single-digit and a two-digit number? (for example, 16 + 7 or 21 – 4)

model their problems with base ten blocks or cubes?

level 2

work out addition and subtraction problems involving two- or three-digit numbers? (for example, 150 + 135)

work out multiplication problems involving a single-digit and a two-digit number? (for example, 16 x 4)

use a calculator to check their answers?

level 3

work out addition and subtraction problems involving four-digit numbers? (for example, 1197 – 563)

work out multiplication problems involving two-digit numbers? (for example, 16 x 17)

work out two-stage problems? (for example, (34 + 79) x 5)

use a calculator to check their answers and, if they are wrong, find their error and put it right?

level 4

work out multiplication problems involving a three-digit number? (for example, 164 x 7 or 164 x 17)

work out problems involving a decimal number? (for example, 48 x 1.5)

work out harder two-stage problems? (for example, (94 – 79) x 15)

use a calculator to check their answers and, if they are wrong, find their error and put it right?

level 5

Solving Numerical Problems

Applying Operations

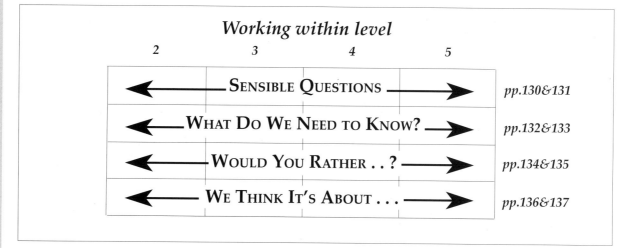

Working within level

	2	3	4	5	
←	SENSIBLE QUESTIONS		→		pp.130&131
←	WHAT DO WE NEED TO KNOW?		→		pp.132&133
←	WOULD YOU RATHER . . ?		→		pp.134&135
←	WE THINK IT'S ABOUT . . .		→		pp.136&137

The activities in this section are different from those in the rest of the book because they are not arranged around the six modes of working. This is not to say that children should not be using these modes when solving word problems. But rather than starting with a particular mode in mind, the children should be encouraged to select the mode that they think will best help them solve the problem.

Two types of problems are focused on here: 'making-sense' problems, and problems of scale.

'Making-sense' problems (*Sensible Questions* and *What Do We Need to Know?*)

The traditional approach to word problems is to take a particular arithmetical skill or number bond and wrap it up in different contexts. So multiplication problems would often be about trays of cakes or packets of biscuits. This approach can have two unexpected and undesirable outcomes:

● Children come to think of mathematics as only being applicable to stereotyped situations, even when these involve everyday objects, and find it difficult to transfer their learning to a wider context.

● They do not try to make sense of the situation. They assume that the operation they should use will be signalled through the wording of the problem, or the size of the numbers involved ('the numbers are small so it must be a multiplication'), or by the fact that they have just done a few pages of multiplication calculations.

The approach we have taken here is to encourage children to try and make sense of the whole context of the problem. There is no particular operation children should use, and sharing different possible methods with each other will help them engage with the problem, rather than treating it as a spot-the-operation trick.

Problems of scale (*Would You Rather . . ? and We Think It's About . . .*)

The other problems offered here are of the kind where the size and scale of the numbers is beyond most people's ability to understand — they are unlikely to have a good 'feel' for the numbers. (Can you really imagine what a crowd of 25,000 people looks like?)

In such circumstances, children need to check their solutions for reasonableness — not in terms of whether the final numbers make sense, but in terms of whether the method adopted has been carefully thought through.

We offer two suggestions here. The activity 'Would You Rather . . ?' will, we hope, provoke children's curiosity — 'Would you rather have a column of £1 coins as tall as you, or a collection of 20p pieces as heavy as you?'

The activity 'We Think it's About . . .' is focused on more realistic situations — for example, knowing how much water a school uses in a day. Information such as this is often interesting in itself and can also lead on to valuable work on energy conservation, comparisons with other countries, and other social issues. Increasingly our world is presented in mathematical terms — just flick through any newspaper. Even from an early age children can be encouraged to begin to develop a critical attitude to this 'mathematisation' of experience. We hope these suggestions may provide a starting point.

SENSIBLE QUESTIONS

Children will experience

◆ considering what sort of calculations make sense in the context of a problem
◆ writing their own problems for others to solve

Equipment

◆ paper and pencil

Getting started

This activity can be done in groups or with the whole class.

Choose a simple calculation, such as 25 – 4. Check that the children can find the answer. Invite individuals to invent a story problem that would require the calculation 25 – 4 to find the answer — for example "I baked twenty five biscuits but four got broken. How many were left?"

Now provide the children with a 'set' of related calculations, such as

$$36 + 6, 6 + 36, 42 - 6, 42 - 36$$

Ask them in pairs to make up several stories to go with each calculation. The pairs should then swap stories and write which calculation they think goes with each story.

Important mathematics to discuss

There is no simple 'trick' to making sense of a story problem. For example, 'more' can mean addition, as in "I won five marbles and then four more", or subtraction, as in "I have eight marbles; that's four more than Jim. How many does Jim have?" Discuss with the children strategies for making sense of the problems and deciding which operation to use — for example, drawing a picture, modelling the situation with concrete materials, or acting it out, can all help.

Questions to ask the children

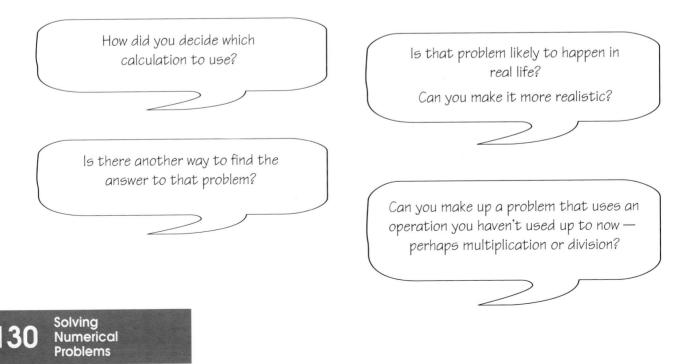

How did you decide which calculation to use?

Is that problem likely to happen in real life?

Can you make it more realistic?

Is there another way to find the answer to that problem?

Can you make up a problem that uses an operation you haven't used up to now — perhaps multiplication or division?

Keeping going

◆ Give different pairs different sets of calculations. Can they answer each others' problems?

◆ Children can make up stories involving more than one operation.

◆ Pairs can make up their own sets of calculations to exchange with each other and write stories for.

◆ Ask children to write 'true stories' and equations about ordinary school activities — "There are 35 in the class and 7 of us have packed lunches. How many eat school dinners?"

Can the children . . .

pose problems involving addition and subtraction of whole numbers?

pose problems involving addition and subtraction of money?

distinguish between those occasions when they need to use addition and those when they need to use subtraction?

level 2

pose problems involving multiplication and division of whole numbers?

pose problems involving multiplication and division of money?

pose problems involving metric units of length, weight or capacity?

distinguish between those occasions when they need to use multiplication and those when they need to use division?

level 3

pose problems involving decimal notation to two decimal places in the context of measurement?

pose problems involving simple percentages?

level 4

pose problems involving decimals and percentages?

pose problems involving fractions and ratios?

pose problems involving negative numbers?

choose whether decimal fractions or vulgar fractions are more appropriate in a given situation?

level 5

WHAT DO WE NEED TO KNOW?

Children will experience
◆ considering, ordering, and selecting information to solve word problems
◆ working cooperatively

Equipment
◆ paper and pencil
◆ scissors

Getting started
This activity can be done in groups or with the whole class.

You will need to have prepared a suitable story problem. This should contain several items of mathematical information, not all of which are relevant to the solution of the question. Each piece of information should be written on a separate slip of paper. There should also be a slip of paper containing a question.

For example, items of information might be:

Rashid was going to visit his grandmother

The train leaves at 10.00 am

The ticket costs £2.50

The journey takes 55 minutes

Rashid's grandmother is 68 years old

The train was 10 minutes late

Rashid arrived at the station at 9.45 am

Rashid's grandmother met him off the train

The question for children to answer is, "What time did Rashid meet his grandmother?"

Ask the children to read out each item of information and discuss which ones are relevant. They should then arrange this information in order to help them solve the problem.

Later, pairs of children can work together, making up similar stories and cutting them up into separate items of information. The pairs should then swap and try and solve each other's problems.

Important mathematics to discuss
There is no one right way of ordering the information — presenting it on slips of paper helps to emphasise this.

Questions to ask the children

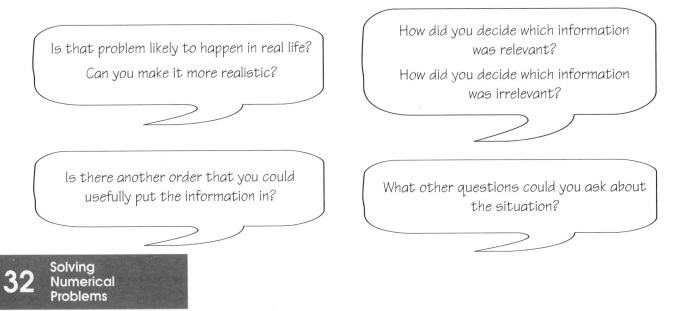

Is that problem likely to happen in real life?
Can you make it more realistic?

How did you decide which information was relevant?
How did you decide which information was irrelevant?

Is there another order that you could usefully put the information in?

What other questions could you ask about the situation?

Keeping going

◆ Give pairs a question such as, "What was the total cost?" Children have to write their own stories to match the question.

◆ Pairs of children write stories for another pair, but before swapping they randomly remove one or two pieces of information. The pair solving the problem has to create any missing information that they need.

◆ Present stories as a whole (not on slips of paper) and discuss how making notes can help sort out a sensible order for handling the information.

◆ Groups of four share out the slips of paper containing the information (it doesn't matter if they don't each have the same number of slips). They can read out to each other what is written on their slips, but not show the other group members. Can they collectively solve the problem?

Can the children . . .

solve word problems involving addition and subtraction of whole numbers to ten?

solve word problems involving addition and subtraction of money?

identify irrelevant information?

level 2

solve word problems involving multiplication and division facts in the 2, 5, and 10 times tables?

solve word problems involving multiplication and division of money?

solve word problems involving metric units of length, weight or capacity?

identify relevant but redundant information?

level 3

pose and solve word problems involving multiplication and division facts up to 10 x 10?

pose and solve word problems involving decimal notation to two decimal places in the context of measurement?

pose and solve word problems involving simple percentages?

create sensible data to replace missing information?

solve problems requiring two operations?

level 4

pose and solve word problems involving decimals and percentages?

pose and solve word problems involving fractions and ratios?

pose and solve word problems involving negative numbers?

solve problems requiring multi-step solutions?

level 5

WOULD YOU RATHER . . ?

Children will experience

◆ dealing with large numbers
◆ checking the reasonableness of answers by considering the methods of calculation used

Equipment

◆ paper and pencil
◆ calculators

Getting started

This activity can be done in groups or with the whole class.

Offer the children a 'would you rather' situation, such as:

"Would you rather have a column of £1 coins as tall as you or a collection of 20p pieces as heavy as you?"

"Would you rather have a present for each day you have lived or one per second for 12 hours?"

"Would you rather have £5 per day for two weeks — or 2p on Day 1, 4p on Day 2, 8p on Day 3 and so on, doubling the amount every day until Day 14?"

Encourage the children to decide which they would choose, and why, before doing any specific calculations. Then set them off to find out which is the better deal.

Important mathematics to discuss

It is impossible to know whether the solutions to these problems are correct simply by looking at the answers — and the numbers are too large for children to have a 'feel' for which ones seem likely. Encourage the children to talk through the methods they used (and different groups may have obtained different answers), to listen carefully to each other's methods and to check these methods as a way of checking the solutions.

Questions to ask the children

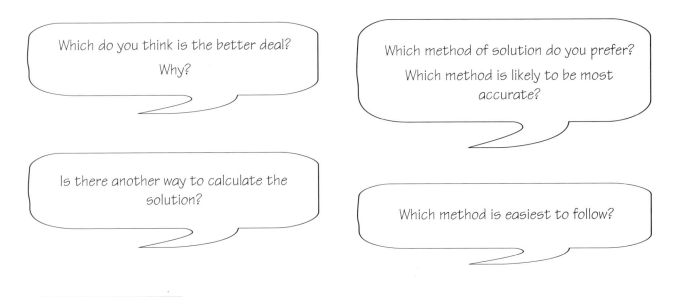

Which do you think is the better deal? Why?

Which method of solution do you prefer? Which method is likely to be most accurate?

Is there another way to calculate the solution?

Which method is easiest to follow?

Keeping going

◆ Pairs can make up their own 'would you rather' situations to exchange with each other and solve.

◆ Further problems are:
"You are being built your own private swimming pool. Would you rather have one containing a million litres, or one as big as five classrooms?"
"Imagine you are starting out as a rock star and want lots of fans. Would you rather have 2,000 fans, or as many as would fill the school playground?"

Can the children . . .

talk about the problem and discuss the mathematics needed to find a solution? devise ways to model a situation, with help where necessary?   *level 2*

try different mathematical approaches? work systematically to find a solution? discuss their work and explain their thinking? *level 3*

find alternative solution strategies to check their answers? present their reasoning in a clear and ordered way?   *level 4*

identify and obtain information needed for a solution? describe a situation mathematically using symbols, words and diagrams, as appropriate? *level 5*

WE THINK IT'S ABOUT . . .

Children will experience

◆ estimating with large numbers in a range of contexts
◆ checking the reasonableness of answers by considering the methods of calculation used

Equipment

◆ paper and pencil
◆ calculators

Getting started

This activity can be done in groups or with the whole class. (Individuals are unlikely to feel confident tackling such problems on their own.)

Offer the children an estimation situation, such as:

"How many people could stand in the classroom? In the school hall? In the playground?"

"How much paper does the class use in a day? How many pages will you fill during your school career? How much paper does the school use in year?"

"How much water does a typical child drink in a day? How much does a child use in a day? How much water does the school use in a year?"

Important mathematics to discuss

It is impossible to know whether the solutions to these estimations are correct simply by looking at the answers — and the numbers are too large for children to have a 'feel' for which ones seem likely. Encourage the children to talk through the methods they used (and different groups may have obtained different answers), to listen carefully to each other's methods and to check these methods as a way of checking the solutions.

Questions to ask the children

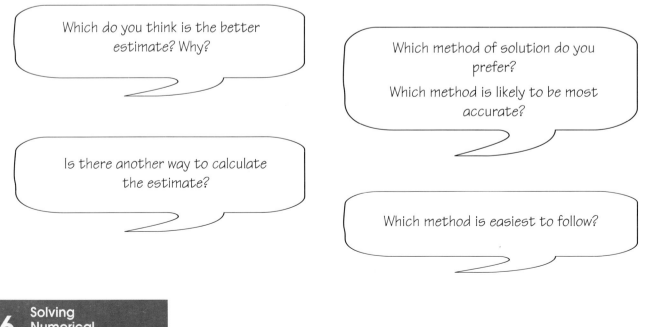

Which do you think is the better estimate? Why?

Which method of solution do you prefer?

Which method is likely to be most accurate?

Is there another way to calculate the estimate?

Which method is easiest to follow?

Keeping going

◆ Pairs can make up their own estimation problems to exchange with each other and solve.

◆ Use opportunities for similar problems as they arise in ordinary school activities — "About how many sheets of paper are there here?", "How many helpings do you think fit in that pan?"

Can the children . . .

make sensible estimates involving addition and subtraction of whole numbers, including money?
make sensible estimates involving numbers to a thousand?
level 2

make sensible estimates involving multiplication and division of whole numbers in the 2, 5, and 10 times tables?
make sensible estimates involving multiplication and division of money?
make sensible estimates involving metric units of length, weight or capacity?
level 3

make sensible estimates involving multiplication and division facts up to 10 x 10?
make sensible estimates involving decimal notation to two decimal places in the context of measurement?
level 4

make sensible estimates involving decimals and percentages?
make estimates involving fractions and ratios?
level 5

RESOURCES

Number Cards

Blank cards and 0-100 cards are available from AMS Educational. They are the same size and material as standard playing cards.

AMS Educational, Woodside Trading Estate,
Low Lane, Horsforth, Leeds LS18 5NY
Tel 01532 580309 Fax 01532 580133

Number Lines

BEAM sells 1m long number lines made of brightly coloured card, with a surface which children can write on with felt-tipped pens and then wipe clean. The 0-100 lines have intervals of just under 10 mm and an unnumbered line with 100 intervals on the reverse.

BEAM, Barnsbury Complex, Offord Road,
London N1 1QH
Tel 0171-457 5535 Fax 0171-457 5906

Fun with Spreadsheets

Eighteen interesting spreadsheet activities — many of them 'real' such as 'Which toy car is best at rolling down a ramp?' The activities encourage children to explore questions by entering measurements on a spreadsheet, and then manipulating them.

by Diana Cobden and Martin Longley
ISBN 0 852167 86 5
Dorset County Council, Jade Manor Court,
West Quay Road, Poole, Dorset BH15 1JG
Tel 01202 221453

Spreadsheet Activities for Key Stages 1 to 3

Spreadsheet activities designed to help children develop a range of mathematical skills. Each activity suggests a 'starter' which can be explored and extended in various ways.

by the Oxfordshire Mathematics Centre and IT
Advisory Team
ISBN 1 85599 01
Oxfordshire Mathematics Centre, Cricket
Road Centre, Cricket Road, Oxford OX4 3DW
Tel 01865 749505

Slimwam 2

This is a collection of six computer programs suitable for children. One of them, 'Monty,' is used in the activity on page 50.

Slimwam 2 is available for BBC, Archimedes and Nimbus.

Association of Teachers of Mathematics,
7 Shaftesbury Street, Derby DE23 8YB
Tel 01332 346599 Fax 01332 204357

Number Games

These 26 strategic number games for the computer were devised by Anita Straker. They encourage a range of skills including mental mathematics, strategic and logical thinking and the making and testing of simple hypotheses. The games include 'Boxes' which is used in the activity on page 8.

This program is available only for the RM Nimbus.

LETSS, The Lodge, Crownwoods, Riefield Road,
Eltham, London SE9 0AQ
Tel 0181-850 0100 Fax 0181-850 0400

Microsmile

The First 31

These 31 programs cover a wide spectrum of mathematics. The games include 'Guess' and 'GuessD' which are used in the activities on pages 2, 8 and 23.

The Next 17

These 17 programs include 'Identify', 'Define', 'Darts' and 'Minimax' which are used in the activities on pages 64, 65 and 92.

11 More

These 11 programs include 'Magnify' and 'Tenners' which are used in the activities on pages 22 and 23.

All these programs are available for the RM Nimbus and Archimedes.

SMILE, 108a Lancaster Road,
London W11 1QS
Tel 0171-221 8966 Fax 0171-243 1570

Acknowledgments

The activity on pages 78 and 79 is based on an activity in *Fun with Spreadsheets* by Diana Cobden and Martin Longley, produced by Dorset Education Department. We wish to thank them for kindly letting us use their activity in this book.

We would also like to thank the following teachers and schools for trialling the activities in this book, and suggesting helpful changes:

In Tower Hamlets

Kirsten Dwyer, Cate Lyle and Halley Primary School

Sandra Roberts and Shapla Primary School

Elizabeth Setterfield and John Scurr Primary School

Peter Overton and Olga Primary School

Jackie Trudgeon and Canon Barnett School

Hasan Chawdhry and Globe Primary School

Helen Warner, IT Inspector

Elsewhere

Diana Cobden, Mathematics Adviser, Dorset

June Loewenstein, Mathematics Consultant, Surrey

BEAM Director   Sheila Ebbutt

BEAM Editor and Designer   Fran Mosley

BEAM Project devised by   Lynda Maple and Anita Straker

About BEAM

BEAM is a curriculum development project for primary mathematics. We publish a range of materials and run an in-service programme for teachers in primary, nursery and special schools. Our aims are to:

- develop teachers' understanding of mathematics
- help them find a way of teaching which fits with the way children learn mathematics
- provide support for the implementation of the national curriculum for mathematics

For further information on BEAM publications or courses please get in touch with Sheila Ebbutt at:

BEAM, Barnsbury Complex, Offord Road, London N1 1QH
Tel 0171-457 5535 Fax 0171-457 5906